I0138668

REMEMBERING
the FUTURE

REMEMBERING
the FUTURE

A Collection of Essays,

Interviews, and Poetry at the

Intersection of Theology

and Culture

The Other Journal
2004–2007

edited by

**Chris Keller and
Andrew David**

CASCADE *Books* • Eugene, Oregon

REMEMBERING THE FUTURE
A Collection of Essays, Interviews, and Poetry at the Intersection of Theology and Culture: *The Other Journal* 2004–2007

Copyright © 2009 Wipf and Stock Publishers. All rights reserved. Except for brief quotations in critical publications or reviews, no part of this book may be reproduced in any manner without prior written permission from the publisher. Write: Permissions, Wipf and Stock Publishers, 199 W. 8th Ave., Suite 3, Eugene, OR 97401.

Cascade Books
A Division of Wipf and Stock Publishers
199 W. 8th Ave., Suite 3
Eugene, OR 97401

www.wipfandstock.com

ISBN 13: 978-1-4982-1121-5

Cataloging-in-Publication data:

Remembering the future : a collection of essays, interviews, and poetry at the intersection of theology and culture: *The Other Journal* 2004–2007 / edited by Chris Keller and Andrew David.

xii + 196 p. ; 23 cm.

ISBN 13: 978-1-55635-908-8

1. Christianity and culture. I. Keller, Chris. II. David, Andrew. III. Title.

BR115.C8 R41 2009

Manufactured in the U.S.A.

Contents

Contents

Acknowledgments

The Other Journal is a product of the hard work and creative vision of dozens of volunteers. Over the years our vision has been nurtured and critically sharpened by many friends and colleagues, and we are especially grateful to Seth Rash, Ryan James, Jon Stanley, April Folkertsma, Andy Barnes, Jennifer Dwyer, Dan Rhodes, Ben Suriano, Becky Crook, Ashley Bromstrup, Julie Naegeli, Scott Sammons, John Totten, Jon Bergstrom, Paul Jaussen, Sean Jackson, and Christina Maria Desvaux.

I am grateful to Brian Munz, our co-founder, who has spent many sleepless nights imagining and constructing the countless incarnations of the journal. Without him, there would be no *The Other Journal*.

I am grateful to my wife, Ali Keller, and Brian's wife, Kimberly Munz, who have patiently advocated for, critiqued, and dreamed with us about this venture since its embryonic stage.

I am grateful to my co-editor, Andrew David, for his enthusiasm and much-needed editing zeal; he came on board at just the right time, and his work on this anthology and beyond has been invaluable.

Finally, thank you to our readers who have allowed us to grow slowly and steadily. We hope you appreciate this offering, one that, finally, is in print.

Chris Keller
Editor-in-Chief
The Other Journal

Preface

The Other Journal (*TOJ*) was founded in 2003 as an online quarterly dedicated to the exploration of important cultural movements, trends, and pop-phenomena through the lens of Christian faith. Chris Keller, a psychotherapist and recent seminary graduate, and Brian Munz, a writer and web developer, formed the journal as a means for young Christian scholars to network and share their work, work that was born from a theological conviction that authentic, redemptive Christian practice requires double-vision, that is, thoughtful engagement with both the biblical tradition and the cultural moment.

In 2004, *TOJ* opened the editorial gates for interviews and essays from senior scholars and seasoned social activists. Because of the overwhelmingly positive response from the *TOJ* community, this shift from graduate student essays to the work of leading Christian thinkers was accompanied by rejuvenated efforts to locate and publish creative writing that imaginatively considered the convergence of faith and culture.

TOJ is and has always been a labor of love, sustained by the hard work, passion, and skills of its volunteers. Each volunteer—whether a scholar, artist, film buff, editor, or creative writer—has contributed significantly to the direction of each incarnation of the journal.

Remembering the Future consists of content from 2004–2007 that best captures the soul of the journal. The layout of the anthology progresses thematically and organically, providing the reader with a panoply of stylistic and thematic directions that express the mission of *TOJ*: to explore the intersection of theology and culture.

Although *TOJ*'s emphasis on the relationship between theology and culture occurs in the context of a broader movement of Christian cultural criticism and activity, *TOJ* is unique in that it is not a vehicle for any one agenda. It features voices from the emergent movement, but is not an emergent publication; its founders claim a progressive evangelical trajectory as central to their spiritual heritage, but it is not an evangelical publication; and although it relies heavily on the work of leading theologians from Methodist, Presbyterian, and Anglican churches, to name a few, it is not a mainline publication.

Then what is *TOJ*? It is a prophetic publication in that it attempts to unmask the political, economic, and cultural logic that is driving Western society and shaping the church into an image of itself. It is a curious publication in that it assumes that God is active beyond the walls of the church, often in the places we are taught to least expect. And it is a passionate publication in that it is sustained by a desire to love God and neighbor, to see that God's will be done on earth as it is in heaven.

Remembering the Future invites the reader to look deeply at the key issues of our day in light of the vast resources of the Christian tradition and to look deeply at our Christian tradition in light of the key issues of the day. Our hope is that such double-vision will help us watch for the work of God's Spirit and thereby lead us toward a more authentic Christian faith and a more potent redemptive presence in our world.

chapter 1

A Few Suggestions for an Insubordinate Idea

by Luci Shaw

You've untangled yourself from my hair,
floating behind me on one very thin strand.

So I loose you to the early air, not wanting teething
or sleepless nights, hoping you'll find your way

at a young age. So—little enthusiast, full
of possibilities—don't die. Photosynthesize.

Grow your own green leaf or several. Bleed
oxygen for my breathing. Absorb my CO_2:

together we may balance the atmosphere.
Drop a seed into the humus of told thoughts.

Offer a nipple for a neighbor's thirst
or a flake of desert manna with a honey sweetness.

Oh, small particulate of the mind, why not
turn to lightning in a bug that signals, *Stop. Go.*

Start a blaze hot as fatwood. Fling
a glitter of ash over the ocean, pocking it like rain.

Ignite a burning bush. Transfix the universe. Then,
having found a mind of your own, come home.

Burrow my brain. Be one of a neuron couplet
that breeds a host of your own kind.

chapter 2

Revolutionary Remembering

An Interview with Miroslav Volf

by Jon Stanley

ISSUE #9 OF *The Other Journal* (*TOJ*) explored whether contemporary pop-revolutions are "signs of a coming cultural sea-change" or "pop-parodies easily co-opted by the powers that be." Yale theologian and award-winning author, Miroslav Volf helped us advance this debate by first reflecting on the relationship between Christianity and revolution and then discussing other topics such as the practice of transformative theologizing, the necessity among evangelicals for a more holistic understanding of salvation, the relationship between human flourishing and the "sustained pursuit of the common good," the "*Hiltonization* of culture," and the role that right remembering plays in working toward justice, forgiveness, and reconciliation.

———— ☙ ————

The Other Journal (*TOJ*): As you know, the theme we are discussing in this issue of *TOJ* is pop-revolution—the use of revolutionary images, symbols, and rhetoric in popular culture. In our introduction to the issue, we suggested that before getting into the analysis of particular pop-revolutions or the phenomena of pop-revolutions in general, we would have to address the broader question of the relationship between Christianity and revolution. What is your understanding of the Christian account of revolution? And to what extent is Christianity revolutionary? That is to say, to what extent does it aim toward the disruption of the status quo and the radical transformation of any and all aspects and sectors of society?

Miroslav Volf (MV): I think it really depends on what we understand by *revolution*. Your second sub-question is probably relevant here. My conception of revolution comes from intimate work with and study of Karl Marx. In this regard, I think that revolution ought not to be identified with something like a mere "disruption of the status quo" or "significant social change." That would be, in my judgment, far from an adequate account of revolution. And if one has a more robust notion of revolution, then I think one might have to say that the Christian faith is in a profound sense rather revolutionary, but this revolution is an eschatological one. The Christian faith is certainly about the coming world of love, and for that, a radical transformation of reality is necessary. No mere translation of souls into some heavenly bliss will suffice; what is needed is the transformation of all reality so as to become the world of perfect love!

Now, whether and how eschatological transformation translates into historical transformation is a very important question. My sense is that *disruption*—a term not dissimilar to *interruption*, which the political-theologian Johann Baptist Metz has used—is not a truly Christian category. Rather, as Jürgen Moltmann noted in response to Metz, the proper Christian category is that of *conversion*. Disruption and interruption are merely negative categories. Conversion is a fundamentally positive category. Now, this means that this negative element of disturbing the status quo must be understood as fully in the direction and service of that toward which the conversion is happening. So transformation seems to me a much better term for this process as a whole. In that sense, does Christianity aim at converting the present reality into something akin with the coming revolution of God's kingdom? I would say, very definitely so! And if not, then it isn't Christianity as it has originally been envisioned!

TOJ: You have spoken of the eschatological revolution, firstly, not in terms of the translation of souls into a heavenly bliss, but as a radical transformation of all reality into the world of love, and secondly, as a future transformation by God that is related to our transformative work in the present. Now, to those who might be skeptical of your understanding of the scope of the eschatological revolution and its relation to the transformation of reality within history, and who might therefore be suspicious of Christian efforts not explicitly concerned with the salvation of souls, what biblical or theological themes would you highlight in order to persuade them otherwise?

MV: Well, I think there is certainly a plethora of biblical resources from which one can draw. The prophetic tradition is a very significant resource, where the goal is not simply the salvation of souls but the transformation of society, the transformation of the entire way in which we together live as individuals and communities before God. The same I think is true of Jesus's ministry. His healings and miracles, in the context of the announcement of the Kingdom of God, play such a significant role that I think it is appropriate to speak of the transformation of reality as salvation, which again, is a much broader notion of salvation than merely the salvation of souls. When we think about the Apostle Paul, it is often forgotten that he too displays a significant concern for the poor throughout his ministry. And then of course the vision in the book of Revelations is a fundamental resource, where the City of God (i.e., the New Jerusalem) comes down from heaven to this earth and transforms it. "Behold, I create every thing anew, a new heaven and a new earth." So to me these are the lines I would work within—that God creates and therefore tends to creation and ultimately consummates it. We see this in the prophetic tradition, we see this in Jesus's ministry, we see this in Paul's ministry, and we see this in the expectation of the eschatological fulfillment in Revelations. All of this seems to me to speak robustly in favor of a very broad understanding of salvation, which certainly includes a salvation of souls—the relationship of the individual to God. The salvation of souls as the reconciliation of individuals to God is certainly fundamental, but it is a piece of a much larger account of salvation.

TOJ: That is very helpful. So helpful in fact, that I have to ask why North American evangelical theology fails to operate with the broader understanding of salvation that, as you have shown, runs so deeply in the biblical tradition? Evangelical theology seems unable to get over the dualism that pits eschatological salvation against historical salvation, and personal salvation against social salvation. Why is this so?

MV: By the way, it is not just evangelicals who hold to that kind of soteriological dualism. One can see this in [Martin] Luther's two-kingdoms doctrine. Though he was very much opposed to abandoning the world to its own devices, as is the temptation of some forms of evangelicalism, he nonetheless operated with a split between how God works in relationship to the soul and how God works in broader reality. I think evangelicalism, especially older-style evangelicalism, operates with a contrast between personal salvation and social change. To remedy this, it is essential for us to consider the unity of God's work in the whole of humanity and creation, and that brings us to the all-important notion that God is a God of love. In regard to creation, God is a God of love. And therefore in regard to creation gone astray, the God of love is also the God of grace. And that applies to all realms of our lives: not just to our being in right standing personally with God, but also with our being in right standing with one another; not just for us loving God and being loved by God, but also for us loving one another and being in relationships of *shalom*, in relationships of peace with one another. God's love and God's grace ought to permeate all our lives in distinct ways. When this happens, then the Gospel is productive, I think, and it is furthering an integral transformation of reality.

TOJ: So if coming to terms with the unity of God's work is essential for overcoming the dualisms that plague not only evangelicalism but, as you have suggested, many other theological traditions, how would you suggest that we begin to trace the ways this theme permeates and applies to all areas of life?

MV: Grace is not just for the life of the soul [. . .], grace is for all reality. Now, of course, when we say that, we are required to make some very careful distinctions. Here, I think something like what Karl Barth has done with the notion of *analogy* is quite helpful. The pattern in which God relates to us as individuals has analogies in the way we should think of the relations between people in civic community, for instance. These two sets of relations are neither identical nor completely different; they are analogous. God's relation to us in Christ cannot simply be transposed onto all spheres of life. But analogies can be drawn. These analogies can then provide helpful insight into the ways that God's grace can be made fruitful for all areas of life.

TOJ: Judging from your example, is it fair to say that you see the Barthians in North America as providing the most helpful resources for evangelicals struggling with the question of how Christian faith relates to the life of society?

MV: Well, that depends upon what Barthians you are talking about and what particular Barthians do with Barth's work. In my own work (say, *Free of Charge*), I have drawn heavily on Luther—a particular reading of the early Luther—even though I am critical of his two-kingdoms doctrine. I certainly see Barth's legacy as one significant model within Protestantism of how to deal with issues of the common good, for instance, and not only that, but how to deal with issues of the common good from the heart of the Christian faith. In some sense, political theologians like Moltmann are also in that broad tradition, even though Moltmann understands his own work in part as providing an alternative to Barth.

TOJ: With each issue of *TOJ* we strive for contemporaneity, to have our finger on the pulse of what's happening now culturally and politically, and to examine these events, issues, and trends from a theological point of view. This issue is no exception. Martin Heidegger famously said that each generation of philosophers is faced with one issue that they must think through for the benefit of future generations. If there is wisdom in this statement, then I assume that it applies to theologians as well. What would you consider the hinge issue of our time, that is, where do you believe we are most in need of theoretical and practical wisdom today? Or more personally, what issues or themes do you plan to deal with in your research and writing over the next few years?

MV: It's very difficult to single out one particular issue. If I were to do it in a more personal way, rather than in a more objective and analytical way, I would probably say that the most significant challenge that we face today—a challenge with which many other significant issues are connected, such as poverty, ecological degradation, runaway technological developments, et cetera—is the notion that human flourishing consists in experientially satisfying life. Put differently, one of our main challenges is that we live in a culture of the managed pursuit of pleasures, not of the sustained pursuit of the common good. To me, that is one of the fundamental issues of the day. My horror-image, so to speak, of where we might go as a culture is what I have called in one place the *Hiltonization of culture*—Paris Hilton as a paradigm of what culture becomes.

TOJ: You should copyright that term [*laughter*]. Parenthetically, I heard on the radio the other day that Paris Hilton's "Chihuahua as the hot new accessory" is raising concerns among true dog-lovers. Sadly, so many Chihuahuas are being returned to the pounds because they won't stay put in purses that the Humane Society in Toronto is putting them to sleep in droves. I guess their owners felt that taking care of them was too much of a hassle.

MV: Hmm, I'll think about that. More abstractly, by the Hiltonization of culture I mean a kind of fleeting life of self-interest and the pursuit of pleasure. This seems to me to be the main malaise of contemporary society, which of course is led by very powerful cultural currents and institutional arrangements. So I think one of the key issues for us is to think anew about the nature and character of human flourishing within the context of larger creation. So the project in which I am involved right now is entitled "God and Human Flourishing." What is the relationship between our over-arching interpretation of life and our account of human flourishing? For Christians, that means what is the relationship between who God is and how God is related to creation and what it means for us to flourish?

TOJ: Your most recent book *The End of Memory: Remembering Rightly in a Violent World* delves further into a topic that seems to run throughout your work, including your previous award-winning books, *Exclusion and Embrace* and *Free of Charge*, namely, the relationship between memory and hope. How does your work with memory and hope connect with, and indeed flow out of, the larger picture of the relationship between God and human flourishing that you have just described?

MV: To me, this is really related to what we were talking about earlier, namely, that God is the lover of creation! Creation comes to be because of the delight of God in there being creatures other than God and in their flourishing. And in that sense, I believe that reflection on the character of God and reflection on the character of human flourishing belong to-gether. And holding those together results in a style of theologizing for which human flourishing stands in the center. Now, when I say *human flourishing*, I don't mean something merely secular. That's exactly what we have to subvert, the opposition between sacred as something to be lodged in the soul or churches and secular as something that describes the rest of creation. Human flourishing means living as an integral person before God, because only in relationship to God in all spheres of our lives can we find full flourishing as human beings. And I suppose this moves us to the question of memory and hope.

TOJ: Sure, let's go with it.

MV: I have written my most recent book on memory, but memory itself is part and parcel of a larger way of being situated in the world, of which hope is a part. The right remembering of wrongs which we have suffered is predicated on certain hopes of what will happen in the future. The title, *The End of Memory*, already contains within it a reference to the future, because the *end* means the purpose and goal of remembering as well as kind of a terminal point of memory. So hope is already present in remembering. How is it that we remember rightly? Well, we remember rightly when we remember in hope for the day in which all people will be reconciled before God. So relearning the forgotten language of hope for our lives and for the life of society is really an essential moment, or element, of being able to remember rightly.

TOJ: What would you say to Christians, including Christian theologians, who tend to minimize the significance of memory, particularly the memory of wrongs suffered?

MV: It is not hard to see how memory is significant for our personal and cultural lives. Without memory, our lives lose the richness and texture we are meant to enjoy as human beings. You know, sometimes I use the example of a stringed instrument. When you play a musical note, copresent in every tone are also subtones. The same is true also of our pasts. The past needs to resonate in the present in all its tonality. And when it does, the present then acquires a richer texture. No memory, no rich identity. Or think of our Christian rather than personal or social identity. Every time we confess our faith, we remember the death and resurrection of Jesus Christ, and in that sense we become identified with Christ as the people of the resurrection. So you can very well say, quite simply, "no memory, no identity," and particularly "no Christian identity"! Hence, memory is absolutely fundamental for Christians, as fundamental for Christians as it is for the Jews.

TOJ: You mention that memory is as fundamental for Christians as it is for Jews. Yet it is primarily the Jewish writers that have championed the value of memory, particularly the relationship between the remembering of wrongs and the pursuit of justice. Why hasn't this theme been as present in Christian rhetoric in the past fifty years or so?

MV: That's a very difficult question. I am not fully sure why that is the case, but I think it may have something to do with the place of justice in both of these great faiths. The more there is an emphasis on justice, the more there will be an emphasis on memory, on remembering truthfully. It seems to me that for Christians, both justice and memory are inserted into a larger whole—the reconciliation and creation of the world of love. Justice is certainly a part of this larger whole, but it is directed toward and serves the establishment of the world of love. And remembering, if I understand things rightly, is also directed toward a goal, and that goal is not simply protection (which is very significant), and it is not simply justice (which is also very significant), but it is reconciliation between those who are estranged on account of wrongdoing. Now, the goal of reconciliation may have certain relativizing effects upon remembering, and if it does, then that's really troubling. That's why it is important for Christians to emphasize that we need to go through remembering in order to get to reconciliation. However, Christians have, at least in the recent decades, oscillated between being sentimental and punitive. We need to overcome this oscillation between, on the one hand, "Oh, it doesn't matter," you know, "it's OK," and so forth, simply shrugging off what has happened, and on the other hand, kind of an implacable retributive stance. We need to find the road toward forgiveness, which entails firstly naming the wrongdoing that has happened and remembering that wrongdoing as it has happened, and secondly, not counting that wrongdoing against the wrongdoer and finding ways to live together. In my book, I have articulated the larger framework in which memory, particularly the memory of wrongs suffered, finds its true meaning. In this way, it should serve as corrective both to those Christians who fail to understand that memory should always serve the goal of reconciliation and to those Christians who fail to understand that without memory true reconciliation is impossible.

TOJ: In your book *The Future of Hope* you distinguished between "hot cultural memories," which have the power to provide vision and direction for society, and "cool cultural memories," which are fleeting and disposable.[1] It seems difficult to maintain hot memories in the midst of a culture that has become Hiltonized. How can we be people of memory in a fast-paced, consumer-oriented society that encourages us to forget so that we can focus our attention on the next new thing?

1. See Volf and Katerberg, "Introduction," x–xi.

MV: I think that's right. We live in a very fast-paced, consumer-oriented culture in which we are always after the next thing. And I think what we need to do, and to learn how to do, is to practice—and maybe this is going to speak to your issue of contemporaneity—the virtue of non-contemporaneity. This can be expressed in many different ways. I have recently expressed this by noting that prophetic faiths, which I think Christianity is, contain two essential elements. One element is the *ascent to God*, and the other element is the *return to the world*. I think we need to make sure that we have time and space for ascents, and that we create environments in which we can immerse ourselves in tradition and in remembering, and climb regularly to the mountain of God. Otherwise we will end up just swimming in the stream of our fast-paced culture, simply echoing whatever the culture happens to be doing. It takes courage, it takes strength, it takes distance, in order to be able to speak meaningfully to the culture, and if we cultivate the time and space for ascent, then perhaps Christians can truly be that prophetic voice within culture today.

TOJ: One of the things that sets you apart from many contemporary theologians is that your writings clearly demonstrate that while theology is not reducible to autobiography, it is nevertheless always very personal. First, what does this say about your understanding of theology and your role as a theologian? And second, for those who have not yet read *The End of Memory*, would you be willing to share the ways in which this book, and the line of theological reflection it advances, grows out of the details of your own life, out of your own suffered wrongs and your struggle to love your wrongdoers?

MV: Right. You know, *The End of Memory* is probably the most autobiographical of all my books, in the sense that the narrative backbone for the entire book is the story of my interrogations at the hands of the military of then-communist Yugoslavia in the mid-1980s. I was conscripted to be a soldier as a conscientious objector, and then I was interrogated for months and threatened with years of imprisonment because suspicions were held that I was a subversive element—partly because I was a theologian, partly because I had traveled abroad, partly because my father was a pastor, and partly because my wife is American. In the book, I use that story of personal violation—which is still relatively mild compared to what happens to many people in the world today—as a window into issues that we face as we attempt to remember wrongs we have suffered. So my own personal story is an entry point into a topic that is, of course, universal, a topic that I describe in my book as the issue of "the memory of wrongdoing suffered by a person who desires neither to hate nor to disregard but to love the wrongdoer."[2]

Now, the reason I use personal narrative as an entry point is because I think that theology is a way of life, and one way to enact how theology is a way of life and how theology serves a way of life is to write in an autobiographical mode. Of course, there are other ways to do this as well, like writing in a more biographical mode, for example, narrating the lives of saints or the lives of whole communities. Either way, I think it is a very important element in writing compelling and thoughtful theology, that is, if one understands theology as I do, as serving a way of life, indeed as being and presupposing a way of life.

TOJ: I don't see many other theologians working with the understanding that theology should serve "a way of life." In that sense, your transformative style of theologizing makes you something of a prophet among your peers.

MV: I don't want to suggest that what I'm doing is the only way in which one can engage in transformative theologizing. By no means! What is essential for theology today, essential for doing theology well today, is explicit engagement with the great issues of the day, shining the light of faith on the great issues we are facing. I think way too much theology today is devoted to the project of analyzing aspects of third-rate contemporary thinkers rather than illuminating great issues with the light of faith and suggesting a way of dealing with them, a way of struggling faithfully before God with those issues. That's risky, of course, because you are not just analyzing what others say, but offering concrete proposals. And it's risky, especially if you interlay those proposals with your own personal story! However, I think this is the direction theology needs to go. I am afraid that theology is going to become irrelevant if we stick simply to the analysis of other theologians' or other philosophers' work.

TOJ: You are clearly a theologian who is willing to risk. And you have certainly done so in *The End of Memory* by being transparent about your

2. Volf, *The End of Memory*, 9.

abuse at the hands of your interrogators. Victims of abuse (of many forms) often report that writing their narrative is both particularly difficult and surprisingly healing. In what way did the practice of writing itself contribute to your own process of engaging the past in the service of love?

MV: Writing about my abuse has certainly been therapeutic in some sense, but I think in many ways one has to have done a work of therapy (properly understood), before writing can even start. But writing itself is a part of a process and it has provided me a way of thinking through and naming particular realities in my life, and challenging myself to live a particular kind of life. I have said a number of times that after I wrote *Exclusion and Embrace* I would sometimes find myself in a situation where I was being wronged and I would hear this small still voice saying, "But you argued in your book … " and a certain action or a certain door was closed for me. So for me there was power in theological argument, which simply illustrates that theology does serve a way of life. Theology has a bite, and it ought to have a bite of that sort!

TOJ: So far we have talked a lot about a theme that pervades your work, the significance of memory for human life, for the life of society, and for vibrant Christian faith. However, in *The End of Memory*, you move beyond the argument for the significance of memory itself—or perhaps, it would be better to say that you assume it—by introducing the distinction between remembering rightly and remembering wrongly. What is at issue in this distinction, and what does it really mean to remember rightly?

MV: If it is true that we should remember, then the important question becomes how is it that we ought to remember? Memory doesn't simply have a cognitive dimension, that is, it's not simply a matter of whether I remember accurately or not. Memory also has a pragmatic dimension, that is, I always do something by remembering—I construct my own identity, I construct the way in which I relate to the world, and so on. As it turns out, we consistently put memory of wrongs we've suffered to destructive, even deadly, uses. That's why remembering rightly is so significant! You can see this very well in the world today, how memories are invoked to justify particular social and individual projects, some for good and some for ill. This is why I have argued in my book that "the memory of wrongs from a moral standpoint is *dangerously undetermined*."[3] Because memories have a significant role in shaping our individual and social lives and the decisions we make as individuals and societies, it is very important to ask the question, how should we remember? And what does it mean to remember rightly? To remember wrongly means to remember vindictively; it means to remember in ways that deepen the conflict and that are destructive for relationships. Remembering rightly, from my perspective, means remembering in a way that heals what has been broken, that reconciles people who have been estranged. For me, that kind of right remembering is guided by the great vision of reconciliation, which was realized in Jesus Christ and which will finally be completed in the world to come.

TOJ: Earlier, you suggested that contemporary Christianity oscillates between being sentimental and punitive. Sadly, these two options simply seem to mimic the conventional wisdom available in our culture today for dealing with injustice and wrongdoing—the weak-hearted forgive and forget, and the hard-hearted never forgive. How does the notion of remembering rightly provide us with a third way?

MV: We need to find, if you want, a middle ground between the attitudes you are describing. For me, that middle ground is defined by what I consider to be one of the most striking features of early Christianity. It consists in holding two things together—naming evil as evil, and at the same time, trying to overcome evil by doing what is good, trying to condemn the evil deed and love the evildoer. There are many ways in which one can see this as a central feature of Christianity. This is involved for instance in any act of forgiveness. As I have mentioned earlier, when I forgive, I name the wrongdoing as wrongdoing, and yet at the same time, I do not let it count against the wrongdoer. What I have done in *The End of Memory* is to apply this basic stance toward wrongdoing and wrongdoer to the question of memory. I propose a way to practice remembering in such a way that memory serves to name the evil and is a means toward reconciliation!

TOJ: The notion of forgiveness you have just described (as including both the naming of evil as evil and the overcoming of evil with good) seems to run parallel with your account of the relationship between judgment and reconciliation, which you suggest is most properly understood in terms

3. Ibid., 34.

of a judgment unto reconciliation. What has informed your view of judgment, and what is at issue for right remembering?

MV: The connection between judgment and reconciliation is fundamental. This connection is present both in the cross of Christ and in the final judgment. In the cross of Christ, there occurs a judgment against sin. At the same time, I think Barth was right when he spoke of Jesus Christ as "a judge who is judged in our place," so that the judgment on the cross serves, and is understood precisely in terms of, reconciliation! Judgment is not some independent act standing on its own, rather it's part and parcel with the process of reconciliation. The same holds true of the last judgment. Certainly, the last judgment includes the naming of sin and evil, but that naming itself is exercised in the context of grace and in the context of reconciliation. That's why I think that the transition between the world as it is to the world that is to come has two significant components. One component is judgment, and the other component is grace, which includes the embrace of the former enemy. Only in this way can the last judgment, this transition from the world as it is to the world to come, be precisely that, a *last* and *final* judgment. If it were merely a judgment, but not a movement toward the other person in grace, then a world of love would not be able to emerge and judgments would continue. But the creation of the world of love is really the goal of God's dealing with humanity in the Christian tradition. God is love. And the world to come, as Jonathan Edwards has so very eloquently said, is "the world of love."

TOJ: OK. If I am following you correctly, your account of what transpires between perpetrator and victim in the last judgment—making way for the transition from the world as it is to the world of perfect love—has profound implications for what it means to remember rightly. Yet it also seems to have profound implications for the second major idea you advance in your book, the notion of non-remembrance, that is, that suffered wrongs will simply not come to mind after the process of reconciliation has taken place. Why does the notion of non-remembrance feature so strongly in your account of forgiveness and reconciliation?

MV: In terms of non-remembrance of wrongs suffered in the Christian tradition, I ask a very simple question: How is it that for centuries, for millennia really, Christians have associated forgiveness with non-remembrance, but after the 1960s we find it difficult to do so? Now, have we learned so much more in recent decades that we can discard what has been maintained in the Christian tradition for centuries (and indeed, in the Jewish tradition as well, as the theme of non-remembrance has roots in the imagery around atonement and God's dealing with the sins of the people within Judaism)? My answer is, well, let's pause to think whether this long tradition ought to be simply discarded or whether it contains something that is fundamental, fundamental to the way that God relates to us and fundamental for the way in which we should relate to each other. That's the question that I've posed for myself as I sought to think afresh about the possible role of the non-remembrance of wrongs in the process of reconciliation. One way in which I explore the plausibility of the notion of non-remembrance in the book is by looking at the relationship between non-remembrance and salvation, human identity, and moral responsibility.

TOJ: Let's pick up on moral responsibility, as it is perhaps the most controversial. You have already described the strong link between remembering wrongs and the pursuit of justice and reconciliation for victims. If there is a moral obligation to remember wrongs rightly, how does your notion of non-remembrance avoid the charge that it is morally irresponsible?

MV: If one thinks of non-remembrance as a way to deal with the problem of wrongdoing, then of course it will encourage moral irresponsibility. You'll simply forget the wrong. It would be like an ostrich hiding its head in the sand assuming that everything is going to be OK. But the idea that I am advancing is that non-remembrance occurs as a consequence of the world-made-whole, of relationships in the world having been set aright. In this way, remembering is part and parcel of moral responsibility attending to the wrong. This is why I have stated very carefully that what I am proposing is "the not-coming-to-mind of wrongs suffered after justice has been served and after entrance into a secure world of perfect love."[4] Once the world has been set aright, then the question becomes, why should we hold on to those memories? Or as I put it in the book, "What function would those memories serve in a secure world of perfect love?"[5] So I would certainly not want to suggest that we should practice something like a Nietzschean form of non-remembrance, which is precisely an expression

4. Ibid., 203.
5. Ibid., 207.

of unconcern for justice and an abdication of moral responsibility. Naming the wrong as wrong is an essential moment in the healing of the world; therefore, remembering wrongs is also an essential element of healing the world. Now, the question becomes, once that healing is achieved, must we go on remembering? Or can we give each other a gift of not having the wrongdoing inscribed on the forehead of the wrongdoer every time we see the wrongdoer? I would say that we can give this gift, because he is not simply the wrongdoer, but the forgiven wrongdoer. That is why, as I have said elsewhere, the non-remembrance of wrongs suffered "appropriately crowns forgiveness."[6]

TOJ: You have also argued that the idea that we will remember wrongs eternally runs the risk of truncating redemption. In what way is the non-remembrance of suffered wrongs in the world to come consistent with the richest account of redemption that we can imagine?

MV: It would seem to me that if we remembered all the wrongs that have happened, then to be fair we would have to remember all of them to their full weight. And if we did, the consequence I think would be what I can describe only as a dark cloud of non-redemption hanging over the world of redemption. All evil would be remembered, from the smallest to the largest, eternally! The consequence would be, I think, a strange triumph of evil, in that the evil that has marked the world would continue marking the world eternally. Now, of course, different people have different sensibilities about this, but something very profound within me rebels against the notion that evil can have this glory of always being a feature of the remembered world, which is to say, always being part and parcel with the present world, because a remembered wrong is a present wrong. When we remember an evil we bring it into the present in the form of memory, which means that if we were to remember evil eternally then evil would qualify the world to come. And that seems to me to be a deficient account of the world to come, a truncated redemption, if you will, and something less than the world of perfect love in which perpetrators and victims are reconciled, and evil is overcome with good.

But let me clarify what specifically I mean by non-remembrance. One way to look at it is as a simple deletion of a wrongdoing from the hard drive. In this way, the memory of wrongdoing is gone, pure and

6. Ibid., 208.

simple, removed from operative memory and irretrievably deleted from the hard drive. However, I tend not to think about non-remembrance in these terms. My sense is that if someone did want to remember wrongs that she or her loved ones suffered, she could go off into some corner of heaven and brood over things. But my question is why would one want to do that? Some people suggest that for full salvation to take place it might be enough to reframe the memories. That certainly might be an option. Some of them may be able to be reframed, memories of some events which can be rendered meaningful in a positive sense. But my suspicion is that it won't be possible, that it won't suffice, that it would indeed be abhorrent to try to reframe memories of some other events—memories of horrendous evils, for instance.

TOJ: In the case of horrendous evils, would reframing not be enough to really count as redemption, not enough to really make for a world of love?

MV: That's what I am suggesting. Now, if all evil can be seen as instrumental in serving ultimate good, if it is essentially instrumental for the fact of good, then presumably we could live with the remembrance of all evil. Then we would see evil as this kind of bitter but necessary ingredient in the making of the delicious dish called the world of love. Now, if I were able to say something like that, then I think I may have a different account of non-remembrance. But I am not quite able to say that.

TOJ: Thank you very much for your time and for sharing your thoughts with us. It has really been an illuminating discussion. Any final words? We always provide space in our interviews for any final thoughts, comments, or anything our interlocutors would like to say that our questions did not provide the opportunity for.

MV: You're very welcome. And thank you. No, no final words. This is the beginning of a conversation, not the end.

CHAPTER 3

Raping Eve

Reflections on War Rape, the
Political Process, and Grace

by Dan Allender

WE ARE ENTERING a season in our country that is full of vengeance, acrimony, and truth distortion. It is the political equivalent of rape. It is the ugly and dark side, not only of our political process, but far more importantly, of our selves.

Take for example the assault on Max Cleland, a heroic, highly decorated multiple-amputee who was repeatedly labeled as a coward and turncoat for voting against a bill that was to increase money for troop deployment in Iraq. Cleland is a man who lives with the physical vestiges of his courage for all to see, and yet rather than offering a constructive response to his position, the men and women on Capitol Hill stooped to perverse character assassination. Neither the Republicans nor the Democrats hold the higher ground in this process. Indeed, we have come to believe that the political process cannot be accomplished without assaulting the character of our opponents.

Let me ask an odd question: have you ever googled yourself? For the few uninitiated, the verb *google* means to discover what websites exist that are related to your inquiry. To google yourself means to type your name into an online search mechanism known as a search engine and see if anyone cares whether you exist.

Try it. What you discover may amaze you. I found there is a magician in Texas who shares my name. I wonder if, like my namesake, I can pull this topic out of the hat in a way that surprises you. My topic is rape. Most who read this article are not rapists—neither by way of sexual violations nor by committing profound acts of denigration against another human being's dignity—and so it is a topic that is easy to put aside and ignore.

19

The dilemma is that we are all so horrified by the crime of rape, especially cultural, genocidal, and institutionalized rape, that we see it as *their* problem. And the crime of rape is so big, so diabolical, *we* can do little but feel nauseated. We may struggle with lust, but we don't rape. We may be curt or unkind to a wife or girlfriend, but we are not rapists.

Rape is so awful, we are exculpated. War rape is insanely barbaric. It is like trying to comprehend how an image bearer, a human being, can rise, shower, shave, and then trudge off to work to crank up the furnaces that char the dead bodies of children, women, and the infirm. It is evil incarnate, and most of us will never know that world face-to-face.

But how can we understand the enormity of the crisis unless we find some doorway of commonality? If the reality of war rape initially makes us furious but we remain distant, we allow the tragedy to remain *their* problem. We can only help to the degree that we know we are in as deep and desperate a need of rescue as the victims and the perpetrators of war rape.

Care to know about war rape? If so, google some combination of the words *rape*, *Congo*, and *war crimes*. What you find will turn your stomach. You will read about women who have been raped so viciously and often that their vaginas are perforated, that the wall between their urethra and vagina has blended so that they are unable to restrict the flow of urine. They are their culture's new lepers; their stench of urine marks them as unclean. You will read about fiery sticks being inserted in their vaginas and gun barrels being used to prepare the body for even uglier entries.

Many of these rapes are perpetrated by young soldiers, age twelve years and older. They are done under the watchful eyes of the older sergeants who serve slightly older officers. And these crimes against humanity are carefully executed by warlords who know that sex and violence shame their victims and their perpetrators and keep the mechanism of power in place.

And is it only women who are raped? No, men are raped too. They are seldom raped by women, but they are raped by other men. In many war zones, instead of being raped, men have limbs severed—their hands, feet, ears, tongues, and genitals are cut off. This severs a man from his future and deprives him of a life of gainful labor. It strikes at what is most unique about a man's calling, just as rape is an assault against what is most uniquely feminine.

The goal of rape is to shame the victim into submission through loss of face. Rape is never, has never, and will never be about sex. The pleasure in the violation is only incidentally an ejaculation. The real pleasure is the degradation of beauty.

Most war rapes add the dimension of public exposure; war rape is nearly always gang rape. The violation is intended not only to steal and devour dignity, but also to divide the victim from the larger community and to shatter all forms of relationship now and for the future. Rape is the twenty-first century's form of leprosy. It conquers by dividing, separating the family from the victim, and the victim from her culture. It scars the possibility of bringing forth fruit that would avenge the crime or repatriate the land. It is a diabolically brilliant act of war that conquers a person and a people by ravaging the womb.

It happens in the Congo. It happened in an American prison in Iraq. It is likely happening in every prison in the United States. It even happened in the fraternity I joined in Delaware, Ohio. Several weeks ago I sat on my porch with a friend whose fifteen-year-old daughter was raped by a twenty-two-year-old schoolteacher. He raped her at a pool party. One of the teacher's coworkers captured the rape on a phone with video capacity and sent it to another associate who watched the rape in real time.

If you talk to mental health counselors at Christian undergraduate schools, they will (sometimes off-the-record) tell you that the two most common issues they address are eating disorders and date rape. Look closer, and you will see the same darkness that dehumanizes women in the developing world in your own community, church, and university.

I believe one of the most telling and central wars of the early twenty-first century will be fought over how we name and address violence against women. We are a culture, we are a world that is bent on raping Eve. We hate her beauty; we despise her fruitfulness; and we are caught in cultural webs that at different levels shame, silence, and segregate women from the presence and power of community.

Why does this happen? Why does it happen in our military, prisons, fraternities, and schools? Why does it happen in other forms in many churches?

Like all sin, the answer to this question is utterly irrational. Sin makes no sense even when we can explain it. And something like rape is beyond the pale of mere psychological categories. Why did the teacher seduce, rape, and then broadcast his degradation to others: Is it because he had a poor self-image? Perhaps, but it is so beside the point that it is grotesque and offensive to psychologize his evil. Is it better to say that he raped her because he joined evil? Even for those who don't believe in a personal being of evil in this world, this seems more likely, but to identify the act as evil still does not answer the question.

Perhaps it is wise to ask more fundamental questions about gender violence: What places in our culture are indicative of man's hate for feminine beauty? Why do men in some church communities work to shame and silence women by saying, "You can't preach or teach, but you can share from the pulpit; you can't teach men, but you can share as long as you don't quote scripture or teach what the passage may mean"? In faith communities and in the public square, it is often the men who have wrestled with the role of women in leadership, deciding for women that their leadership roles ought to be limited. Women earn lower salaries than men in the business world, are underrepresented in the political sphere, and often are not invited to offer their perspective about major church decisions. These are the subtle roots of more egregious forms of violence.

Let me state a warning with great passion: Don't use the word *rape* loosely. To say "He raped me" after a particularly ugly conversation trivializes the horror of rape even if it aggrandizes how painful an interaction felt. Don't use the word to describe ugly church decisions with which you differ. To say that a particular church rapes women because the leadership refuses to share power with women demonizes a particular theological perspective and uses an ad hominem argument to escape the complexity of the debate.

On the other hand, the question lingers: Why do we systematically and repeatedly denigrate, divide, shame, silence, and rape women? The answer is our hatred of grace. We hate the warm and inviting arms of unwarranted and unmerited forgiveness that is uniquely revealed through the feminine.

The presence of the feminine is a taste of the tender holy kiss of the gospel. And we are unnerved by the tears and kindness of grace because it invites us to the depths of our humanity. If we are human, we will weep. We will grieve harm and wail like children. We will enter our wounds and desperately cry out for tender care.

Such an inner disposition is at war with war. We can't kill without, at some level, creating distance. The other is a knave. A braggart. A worm. A weasel. A narcissist. We can't kill our brother until he is an enemy. We can't kill others until we have turned their wives and daughters into the refuse of our sperm. But once we have marked another with a label or an assault, our wounds are temporarily banished under their shame.

After a person has been marked as less than human, the next assault seems less horrible and more reasonable. One need only watch the escalation of venom and vulgarity in most presidential races. The American people like to watch the drama of contempt.

The majority of reality television shows are a prime example of this; their competition is characterized by exposure, shame, and rejection. It must arouse something in us to watch cruelty and contempt play out on the screen. If we are willing to watch the election of wife, husband, parents, and corporate president by the fallacious theatrics of reality television, how long will it be before we sell political office through a reality program? As unlikely as that sounds, the fact remains: we seem enamored with drama that exalts the victor and demeans the reject. The more our political structure lives and dies by the sound bite and the media blitz, the more simplistic, efficient, and violent the accusations and counteraccusations will be.

Violence is a cloak that hides the wound of our desperation. How can I aid the woman raped in the Congo? I honestly don't know. What can I do to humanize and bring care to the election process? I don't know. But I know that I cannot even begin to imagine how I can help until I proceed through the nausea to a more fundamental sorrow. I must grieve that I am of a gender that rapes. I must groan about the violence my wife and my daughters face and the harm I have brought them. I must name the smaller violations of gender that are endemic in the evangelical community. I must be able to google *Congo* and *rape* and read my own name in those stories.

chapter 4

Blood

by Luke Hankins

I've drawn blood
from others, in my childhood,
even friends and kin—
slit the heavy garment
of skin or split sinus caves
with the hard hammer of my fist.

Very young, I cried
if my sister hurt herself.
Later, her hot blood slicked
my hammering hand—
that hurt was, more
than hers, my own.
And she wept for me.

chapter 5

The Brothels Are Burning

by Heather Coaster Goertzen

IN LATE 2007, the women of El Alto, Bolivia, received international media attention as a result of their struggle against neighborhood efforts to rid their zones of the red light districts and, by effect, the women's means of survival.

———❧———

"The brothels are burning," read the text message on my phone, "They're beating the girls. The girls need help."

Hoping to preserve the rare peace of a Tuesday afternoon, I had already ignored two calls, but now my phone was displaying this message. I grabbed my purse and keys, walked out the door, flagged down a bus, and started making calls. The girls were apparently safe (for the moment), but the *locales* were being pillaged, and the police had yet to show. We were left to watch the fires rise high into an already smoke-filled sky as brothel by brothel, walls and doors wasted away, and all was gutted and burned. I stationed myself at the Word Made Flesh drop-in center, in the window of our four-story chapel, and called the police (yet again). I waited for other members of our team to arrive (we have strict policies against entering these places alone), as I looked out over Calle Carasco and listened to the roar of the mob below.

The police and fire department eventually arrived, and I watched as they followed the mob down the street, block by block, door by door, fire by fire, ensuring the safety of the people, but otherwise letting the crowds have their way. Communal justice. I felt helpless and angry and afraid. I waited for the girls to knock, for God to answer. I read Habakkuk aloud, called a far-away friend, wrote an e-mail to friends and family, and attempted to pray distracted, interrupted prayers, which took the form of short questions and exclamations.

And I couldn't help but notice that this gang of young men who were tearing through walls with rocks and shouting ¡Sí, se puede! closely resembled the crowds we push through during our ministry visits to the brothel. I'm reminded of Genesis 38, of Judah ordering Tamar burned for her sin and then being exposed as complicit in that sin. It has been rumored that a photo of a police official was found in one of the women's rooms, and I wondered how many of those officers recognized the tearful women at their sides. I wondered how many of those young men had seen the inside of the brothel halls before that night, yet not one man stood against the fire-flinging crowd by acknowledging that "she is more righteous than I."

My husband and our director eventually arrived, and together we walked the flaming streets, encountering friends who found their evening shifts barred by a mob of hate. We encouraged the girls we met to go home, lie low, and be safe. Back at our drop-in center, we welcomed a handful of alarmed women, put on some tea, and attempted to calm one another.

One friend arrived drunk, hysterical. She kept repeating the Lord's Prayer and the Hail Mary, interrupting herself with proclamations that God had come to judge her and the others.

I pulled a chair next to where she was kneeling, put a hand on her back, and attempted prayers of my own: prayers for peace, for rescue. And in the midst of the chaos, our sweet friend and coworker, Eliana, herself a victim of decades of exploitation, offered a quieting, prophetic word: "God isn't judging you. Mas bien, He has saved you. They started burning early in the day. What if they had come at night while you were all inside? No, He's saved you." The cries of panic turned to thanksgiving, and then we left discreetly, a few at a time, sneaking back through the violent night, praying that His salvation would really be known.

In the weeks that have followed, we have watched as doors are retacked to their frames, girls return to work, and protests catch the attention of the international media. We have wondered aloud at our own prayers over the years, prayers asking that these places be torn down and destroyed. We are confused about how those prayers may correlate with the violent reaction of that mob.

The women have united in hunger strikes, speaking vocally about their right to work and feed their children, defending the very violation that kills them—some slowly, some suddenly.

One of the women who has been an important voice in the media has suffered both physical and socio-emotional cancers. I sat next to her in a make-shift funeral parlor a few months back, after the violent, work-related murder of a friend, and listened to her laments: "This isn't right. We can't go on like this. There is no life here." A few weeks later I stood beside her in a circle as we prayed to open our annual Mother's Day party, and I heard her offerings of thanksgiving for Christ's presence in her own life and her pleadings that her friends would also know.

And I watch her now, before the media, saddened that her broken-ness and longings have been overtaken by indignant demands that she be given the right to return to her work.

I know the complications of the situation. I know that the neighbors are right to want their children to be safe, to want their husbands not to have to walk past so many red lights on the way home from work, to see this destroyed. I know that the economy is broken and impossible even for those with a fighting chance. I know that our own desires and attempts to find dignified work for our friends have left us with more questions than answers. The impact of poverty and social structure and family violence and sexual abuse frustrate our best intentions and our most holistic efforts.

I pray for the fullness of a coming Kingdom and the courage and strength to love it little by little. Everything else falls short.

chapter 6

Violence and Christian Social Reconstruction in Africa

On the Resurrection of the Body (Politic)

by Emmanuel M. Katongole

THERE IS A SENSE in which, particularly in the summer, all roads lead to Africa. Visitors are not just rich Americans on safari to visit the stunning and exotic beauty of Africa's landscapes and wildlife. Travelers include health workers going to live in African villages, World Vision teams visiting projects in various countries, and young college students traveling to Africa for the first time as part of missions organized to bring the Gospel to Africa and to serve Africa's poor.

The renewed interest in Africa has been shaped by both evangelical and humanitarian trends. Whereas there has always been an evangelical impulse to spread the gospel to Africa, what we have witnessed in the recent past is a renewed interest in that commitment, led mostly by white American evangelical churches. Every year, particularly during the summer, American evangelical churches send mission teams to Africa to preach the Gospel, plant churches, and set up Bible colleges. These missions are all meant to ensure that Africa is spiritually saved.

But there is also another trend, a humanitarian trend; the West is increasingly focused on responding to Africa's endemic needs of poverty. In 2002, President Bush committed fifteen billion dollars to fight AIDS; Bono has continued to sing about the future of Africa and to mobilize governments and companies to help end poverty in Africa; the G8 are talking debt cancellation; Bill and Melinda Gates have invested millions in a malaria vaccine; Jimmy Carter continues his Habitat for Humanity work in Africa; and Bill Clinton is creating a reconciliation initiative. A mood of optimism about

Africa seems to be in the air, and not only among Washington and the likes of Bono: scholars and economists are also getting enthusiastic—take for example leading economist Jeffrey Sachs and his book *The End of Poverty*.

More recently, evangelical churches have also embraced this humanitarianism, and they are now combining the traditional fervor to preach the Gospel with a humanitarian commitment to end poverty in Africa.

As an African theologian I should be excited about this outpouring of spiritual and humanitarian largesse into Africa from Western churches. The renewed interest in Africa points to the reconstruction and, indeed, the resurrection of the social sphere in Africa. But that is where I find myself deeply concerned about not only the excessive optimism that drives many of these programs, but more specifically by their inability to address violence, one of the most urgent problems in Africa today.

And this troubling issue is compounded by the fact that Christianity itself has been drawn into the unfolding drama of violence in Africa. Accordingly, any meaningful mission in Africa should not begin with a consideration of programs, mobilization, and numbers, but with a humble realization that the church has been and remains deeply connected to violence in Africa. Given this fact, how can we think about reconstruction, social renewal, or indeed resurrection in Africa? This is the question that must be at the heart of every church that is planning a mission to Africa. For when it comes to Christianity and missions, Africa is not a tabula rasa, a virgin missionary territory waiting to be discovered and onto which new, powerful, well-thought-out plans and programs can be written ab initio. The Gospel is not new to the continent. Africa has already had a Christian past. Remembering this past, lamenting this painful past, owning it, and critically searching for a more hopeful future out of it is what Christian reconstruction in Africa should be about.

In this essay I would like to map out this alternate starting point for missions, missions that are grounded in memory and lament and that are committed to finding ways of interrupting the social history in which violence seems to be increasingly accepted as inevitable and as part of the normal way of things.

Rwanda, 1994: An Easter Week of Bodies

A Christian discussion about missions in Africa begins with an open and painful study of the relationship between the church and violence in Africa. That is why 1994 Rwanda offers a natural and productive starting point in thinking about social reconstruction and renewal in Africa. In fact, every time I think about the resurrection of the social body in Africa, I think about Easter of 1994.

In 1994, within a period of less than one hundred days, close to one million Rwandans were killed by their countrymen and women. What makes this event particularly chilling for Christian reflection on peace is not simply the fact that Rwanda was and still is a predominantly Christian country with over 90 percent of Rwandans claiming to be Christians. This in itself is a chilling fact, but the even more frightening detail is that church personnel were actively involved in the genocide:

> Church personnel and institutions were actively involved in the program of resistance to popular pressures for political reform that culminated in the 1994 genocide, and numerous priests, pastors, nuns, brothers, catechists, and Catholic and Protestant lay leaders supported, participated in, or helped to organize the killings. . . . In most communities members of a church parish killed their fellow parishioners and even, in a number of cases, their own pastor[s] or priests.[1]

The story of the Rwandan genocide becomes more unsettling when one realizes that the notorious events of those one hundred days of murder began during the Christian Easter season. April 3, 1994, was Easter Sunday. Rwandan Christians joined Christians everywhere to celebrate the resurrection of Jesus from the dead. On the evening of April 6, President Habyarimana's plane was shot down as he returned from a meeting in Tanzania.

Throughout that Easter Octave (the whole week is but one Easter day) and for the next one hundred days, all one saw in Rwanda were mutilated bodies. What irony that the celebration of the risen and glorified body of Christ—". . . the first born from the dead" and "the one who has torn down the wall of separation," thus creating out of a people who once lived as enemies a reconciled community "in whom there is no more Greek or Jew, male or female"—should simultaneously be marked by the

1. Longman, "Christian Churches and Genocide in Rwanda," 140.

33

butchering of Christians by other Christians in the name of being Hutu or Tutsi!

Lament: On Refusing to Be Consoled

Christian social ethics in Africa must begin with this harsh historical memory. To do so is to begin where the Gospel of Matthew begins, in lament. After Herod had ordered the slaying of the innocent children, Matthew simply notes that the words of the prophet Jeremiah were fulfilled:

> A cry is heard in Ramah
> Wailing, bitter weeping
> Rachel, weeping for her children
> She refuses to be consoled,
> For her children, who are not.
> (Matt 2:18, cf. Jer 31:15)

Beginning with the memory of 1994 not only allows lament of the many innocent Rwandans killed, it also allows Christians to lament the violence that Christianity has unwittingly performed in Africa. For what the ironic contradictions of 1994 Rwanda reveal is that genocide was not an event that occurred outside the peaceful ways and message of Christianity. The genocide happened at the very heart of a Christian story in Rwanda. Thus, lament allows Christians to begin to own the story of Christianity in Rwanda as not only the story of Easter, but also as the story of an endless Passion, of a never ending Good Friday. Moreover, the more one reflects on this fact, the more one realizes that 1994 Rwanda is, in the words of Mahmood Mamdani, but a "metaphor for postcolonial political violence."[2] The Rwandan genocide might have been extreme, but it was neither a unique nor exceptional performance of violence within Christian Africa.

That is why, like Rachel in Jeremiah, Christian social reflection on Africa—indeed any program for social renewal—must resist an easy consolation that would distance the 1994 genocide and label it as unique or as the peculiar story of a distant, far-removed, tragically beautiful country. It is not. It is our Christian story.

Grounding Christian social reflection in the idea and discipline of lament also helps us to name and thus resist other consolations, like the too often sunny projection of the growth of Christianity in the South.

---

2. Muhamood, *When Victims Become Killers*, 11.

Whereas there is no doubt that the number of Christians in Africa is growing and that the future of Christianity might actually lie in Africa and the South, I do not find these projections of the growth of Christianity in Africa in and of themselves comforting. For before the genocide of 1994, missiologists were writing self-congratulatory essays and newsletters about the growth of the church in Rwanda and about Rwanda as the model of "successful" missions and church planting.

One must also resist the consolation of those well-designed programs that boast great numbers of workers, Western dollars, and an ability to mobilize but seek to move toward reconstruction without attending to the past. Rick Warren's program to transform Rwanda into a "purpose driven nation"[3] seems to suffer from this danger. Warren, the well-renowned author of *The Purpose Driven Life* and the pastor of the influential Saddleback Church in California, has designed a comprehensive plan to transform Rwanda. He calls it the PEACE program, which stands for Plant Churches, Equip Leaders, Assist the Poor, Care for the Sick, Educate the Next Generation.[4] To be sure, there is much that is fresh in Warren's vision. It is refreshing to find within the tenets of the PEACE program the directive that the program itself is to be spearheaded by lay mission teams from Warren's church. We find here critical evidence that evangelical Christians are moving beyond the traditional focus on saving souls and are connecting the message of the Gospel to issues of justice, education, and the physical needs of the poor.

The problem (one of many) is that attempts to provide a quick fix for Rwanda do not sufficiently own or deal with the past. Thus, Warren's advice to the pastors: "If the devil gives you problems about your past, remind him of his future,"[5] falls far short of the desperate need for Rwanda and all Christians to recognize the role they played in the story of genocide.

However, Warren is not alone in this desire for a quick fix. A similar posture of reconstruction without memory characterizes many of the Christian missions and nongovernmental organizations (NGOs) who genuinely seek to make a difference in Africa. In this way, we fail to face that the Christian story and mission might be part of the problem. By not owning and engaging the past as part of the Christian story, we might

---

3. Morgan, "Purpose Driven in Rwanda," 32–36.

4. Ibid., 35.

5. Warren, *The Purpose Driven Life*, 91.

easily think that Christian mission only brings to Africa the Good News, Easter, and Resurrection.

Cultivating a discipline of lament is thus a way to re-establish a link between the hope for the future and the memory of a dark past, a past which Christians must learn to name as *our* past and whose pain we can claim as *our* pain, not simply because we are its victims, but its perpetrators. Lament thus cultivates the anger necessary to see that there is something fundamentally wrong with the way the Christian story has been conscripted in the performance of violence. It is through lament that we may begin to appreciate the extent to which violence has become a seductive temptation and a powerful spell for Christians. In other words, cultivating a discipline of lament helps Christians to face Paul's angry rebuke to the Galatian Christians: "You stupid Galatians, after you have had the picture of Christ crucified right before your eyes. Who has cast a spell over you?"[6]

Who Has Cast a Spell over You?
Violence as Inevitable

Whereas the particular circumstances that evoked Paul's rebuke of the Galatians might be different from the situation of African Christians,[7] the fact that Paul refers to their betrayal of the Gospel as a "spell" is quite provocative and has implications for Christianity in Africa. Spells are not easy to discern. It is hard enough to know that one is living under a spell, let alone to discern the particular type of spell. And yet such knowledge is necessary if one is to have any hope in overcoming or exorcising the spell. What this means in terms of the challenges and tasks of Christian social reconstruction in Africa is that missions cannot be driven by a prescriptive agenda (offering programs, guidelines, and an agenda of what the church should do), but must be, first and foremost, about description—which is

---

6. Gal 3:1.

7. Paul had preached to the Galatians a message of grace and of freedom made possible through God's new creation (Gal 6:15). Shortly after his departure from Galatia, some Jewish Christians arrived teaching the Gentile Christians that they were obliged to observe the full requirement of the Mosaic law, including the requirement of circumcision (5:2), the keeping of the Jewish dietary laws (2:11–14), et cetera. Paul writes this angry letter in which he exposes the lies behind the claims of the Judaisers in order to bring the Galatians back to the original gospel.

to say, about naming analytically and descriptively the spells that have led African Christians to assume the inevitability of violence in securing or maintaining the social order.

The fact that by 1994 violence had come to be assumed as inevitable by Rwandan Christians requires no elaborate argument. How else can one explain the willingness by which Christians slaughtered other Christians, priests betrayed their parishioners, parishioners killed their priests, husbands betrayed their wives, and wives betrayed their husbands and children? Nevertheless, it might still be useful to highlight this fact through an example.

Augustine Misago is the Catholic bishop of Gikongoro, in southwest Rwanda. When the killing started, a number of Christians took refuge at his cathedral. At first, they were very well taken care of. When the killings intensified, Bishop Misago, together with the local leaders, requested the refugees to leave the church compound and instead gather at a nearby school compound, where they would presumably get better protection. As it turned out, the move left the refugees in the hands of the Interahamwe militia. In all, about eight thousand people were killed at the school in Gikongoro.

After the genocide, survivors accused Bishop Misago of collaborating with the militia in organizing the massacre. He was imprisoned for two years, has since been released because of a lack of evidence, and has resumed his duties as bishop.

I do not tell the story of Misago to determine his guilt or innocence in the genocide but to highlight his response when he was asked about the Tutsi schoolchildren that were massacred at another school run by the diocese and about why he failed to use his influence as a bishop to protect them.

> What could I do? . . . I do not have an army. What could I do by myself? Nothing. That is elementary logic. . . . When men become like devils, and you don't have any army, what can you do?[8]

Misago's statement appears genuine because it points to the realism through which many of us have come to assume violence as inevitable—and perhaps as part of the normal way we expect societies to operate. However, Misago's apparent *helplessness* points to the clear limits of the Christian

---

8. Gourevitch, *We Wish to Inform You*, 138–39.

imagination. That, in fact, is why Misago's response is very instructive. In making reference to the army and his lack thereof, Misago rightly points to an institution of modern nation-state politics through which the domestication of the Christian imagination has occurred.

A number of points are significant here. First, politics and imagination belong together, and contemporary politics work to shape a particular imagination:

> How does a provincial farm boy become persuaded that he must travel as a soldier to another part of the world and kill people he knows nothing about? He must be convinced of the reality of borders, and imagine himself deeply, mystically, united to a wider national community that abruptly stops at the border.[9]

Second, the shaping of the political imagination does not take place in isolation but through the key institutions of nation-state politics: the army, the police, schools, the market or shopping malls, et cetera. Third, by locating her mission neatly within the framework of nation-state politics, Christianity allows her own imagination to be shaped, determined, and domesticated by the dominant political imagination. Lest this sound both abstract and overly theoretical, I will explore these claims in relation to Africa, with a particular reference to Rwanda.

Politics and the Imagination of Violence: The Church and Nation-Building

One key lesson that I learned from Anthony Giddens's *Nation State and Violence* is that modern nation-states are built on an imagination of violence and the threat of war, an external threat of war. Where African nation-states might differ from their Western counterparts is in the fact that, unlike Western democracies, the imagined enemies of the national project are not outside but within nation-state boundaries.

This difference reflects the colonial imagination of African societies and the way that the category of *tribe* and *tribalism* was employed by the colonial regimes. The colonial policy of divide and rule used the existence of many tribes to its advantage, playing one against the other. And then with the help of colonial anthropology and history, an imagined animosity and conflict between the tribes could be read back into the past as though

9. Cavanaugh, *Theopolitical Imagination*, 1.

warfare had prevailed in Africa before the coming of the Western civiliz-ers. Given this imagined age-old animosity between tribes, this supposed perpetual warfare, colonialism, and its successor institution of the nation-state, could happily announce itself as the salvation whose chief task was to pacify the tribes or to help African societies move from barbarism to the civilization of modern nations.

True, there were variations in how the story of *perpetual warfare* was used by the colonial regimes to shape the politics of various nations. In the case of Rwanda, for instance, the Hutu and Tutsi categories, which preexisted colonialism and had operated as complex social, political, and economic relations of a fluid nature, were read as fixed identities of race. With the use of a powerful mythology, the two races were described (and, with the help of science, *confirmed*) not only to be radically different in capabilities, but in their origins—and thus, the (Tutsi) non-indigenous conquerors were locked in perpetual struggle with the (Hutu) subjugated natives. It is this mythology and the attendant view of the Tutsi as inher-ently superior that guided the colonial reforms of the 1920s and served as the basis of modern Rwanda.

Although the 1959 Hutu Revolution was able to turn the world designed by the Belgian colonialists upside down—power was transferred from the Tutsi elite to the Hutu elite—it never questioned the underlying imagination of Hutu and Tutsi as racially different and as "always at war with one another." Thus, throughout the independence period, includ-ing the so-called peaceful times of Habyarimana's Second Republic, the imagination of perpetual warfare between Hutu and Tutsi served as the foundation of independent Rwanda and expressed itself now and again in periodic outbursts of violence.

During this time, the church in Rwanda, the Catholic church in particular, grew in numbers, strength, and power and became fully incor-porated into the nation-state project. True, the church adopted different postures within this project—it encouraged Christian conversion; it built schools and hospitals; it called for and supported development; it even spoke out against government excesses and made appeals for more democ-ratization. Throughout all of this, however, the Church's self-understand-ing was neatly located within the nation-state project.

Having nicely located its work and self-understanding within this powerful narrative and having invested deeply in the project of building the nation, the church lost any skills of discerning the spell that the mythology of perpetual warfare was casting over Rwanda. When the politics of the day called for revolution, the church joined in and became part of the so-called revolution; when it called for development, the church put her support behind it; when it called for popular democracy and the "final elimination" of the enemy, the church readily obliged. By then, it had lost any skills to name the spell within nation-state politics and the will to say no or to imagine alternatives to violence.

The claim I am making by telling the story of Rwanda is not simply that violence and conflict is part of the story of nations. I am making the stronger claim that for Christians nation-building is a spell, a dangerous spell precisely because we do not recognize it as such. Lamenting events like the 1994 genocide in Rwanda helps us to face this truth. It also forces us into a humble search for hopeful alternatives.

Given the story of nations that Rwanda exemplifies, the alternatives in question will have to come by way of skills and postures by which Christians can learn to interrupt the imagination of violence. But that in itself calls for nothing short of reimagining the church's role and posture within nation-state politics. In this respect, Christians have a lot to learn from the Muslim community in Rwanda.

Interrupting Violence

In contrast to the mass participation of Christians in the Rwandan genocide of 1994, one faith community that was able to provide a bulwark against barbarity for its adherents was the Muslim community on the outskirts of Kigali.

There are many testimonies of the protection that members of the Muslim community gave one another and of their refusal to divide themselves ethnically. In Rwanda, Muslims represent a very small proportion of the population (0.2%) and so their faith is not simply a religious choice: it is a global identity choice. Moreover, that Muslims are often marginalized seems to reinforce a strong sense of community identification, a solidarity that supersedes ethnic tags, something the majority Christian communities have been unable to achieve.[10]

What is striking about this example is not the fact that it occurred in a Muslim community, but the name of the village where this community

10. Prunier, *The Rwanda Crisis*, 253.

was located: Nyamirambo. In the Kinyarwanda language, *nyamirambo* means *a place of dead bodies*. It is unclear to me why the place was so named, but given its surroundings, it is not hard to imagine this dirty slum on the outskirts of Kigali near the central prison as a place that might have been viewed by many as a mortuary, a place of violent crime and lawlessness. Yet it was here, in the place of death, that the minority Muslim community found a home at the margins of Rwandan social, political, and economic life. And it was here that they were able to provide an alternative to the barbarity and violence of Easter week. It was here—and not within the Christian churches—that the true sense of Resurrection came to be embodied.

What made it possible for the Muslim community of Nyamirambo to resist the barbarity of tribalism? Gérard Prunier suggests that it had something to do with their being a minority. They understood themselves as living at the margins of the dominant political culture. If this posed some challenges to them, as I am sure it did, it also gave them opportunities and possibilities that were not available to Christians. Among other things, their marginal existence meant they did not assume that it was their responsibility to make Rwanda work. This is also what gave them the possibility of discovering ways and an identity that defied the dominant self-understanding of being Hutu or Tutsi.

Conclusion: The Resurrection of the Body (Politic)

But what has all this to do with Christian social reconstruction and renewal in Africa? A great deal. First, it shows the urgency of dealing with the issue of violence in Africa as part of the crucial task of social reconstruction. Unless the various programs and agencies interested in the social renewal of Africa face this issue, they may easily find their program thwarted and even conscripted within this enduring legacy of violence.

Second, our theoretical exploration confirms that the genocide was not an isolated expression of violence but reflects the assumptions of violence and conflict that are at the heart of nation-state politics. Accordingly, any programs for renewal, be they efforts to end poverty or to fight AIDS, will always somehow fall short of our expectations for renewal unless these programs are able to confront the underlying issues of the political imagination that shapes African societies.

Third, our analyses also reveals the extent to which Christianity itself has been unwittingly drawn into the political imagination and performance of violence in Africa, and unless this fact is confronted, any Christian initiatives and programs for renewal in Africa will not only remain shallow, they might just be a form of activist consolation.

Lastly, if the mass participation of Christians in the Rwanda genocide during Easter provides an opportunity for lament, the example of the Muslim community of Nyamirambo offers a glimpse at a deeper sense of Easter—namely the resurrection of the body (politic) amidst an ongoing social history of violence. The lessons from this case are numerous. Among others, the most urgent task facing Christian agencies in Africa is not humanitarian intervention, but community building. Moreover, the task is not simply one of church planting, but of building up local ecclesial communities that are characterized by disciplines of memory and lament. This task is not a short-term or parachute mission; it requires a long-term, in fact, a lifelong commitment to and presence in a place, village, or community. Such a presence may of course not seem spectacular or newsworthy, but it has the enduring power of witnessing to an alternative of peaceful presence—an alternative that is able to interrupt, through its exemplary ordinariness, the ongoing performance of violence. This is the kind of presence, the kind of resurrection, and the kind of interruption that the life of an Italian social worker named Toni Locatelli bears witness to, and calls Christian missions into.

Across the Nyabarongo River to the southeast of Kigali lies the small town of Nyamata, with a Catholic parish that was run by Belgian missionaries. During the 1994 genocide, UN forces pushed their way through the militia blockades and airlifted the three Belgian priests and a nun out of the violence. Immediately afterward, the militia descended on the people who had taken refuge in the church compound and killed everyone. Over ten thousand people in all. One can still see the bullet holes and the blood on the ceiling in the church, as well as the mass graves in the back of the church. The most telling sign—and ironically, perhaps the only hopeful sign—about this place is the sole grave to the side of the church. It is the grave of an Italian social worker, Toni Locatelli, who had lived in Nyamata for over twenty years.

When the Rwandan Patriotic Front invaded Rwanda in 1990, systematic killings of Tutsis started around Nyamata. Locatelli protested to the local police and alerted the international media about the sporadic but systematic killings that were going on around Nyamata. As a result, the international media descended on Nyamata and reported the killings. In 1992, the police commander, angered by the presence of the international media, shot Toni Locatelli.

When I think about the challenges of social reconstruction and resurrection in a place like Nyamata, I cannot help but think about Toni Locatelli and the interruption that her life, her presence, her lifelong commitment to Nyamata, and her death embodies.

chapter 7

Giving Evangelicals a Peace of His Mind

An Interview with Charles Marsh

by Dan Rhodes

The Other Journal (*TOJ*): The first question I want to pose to you is regarding your 2006 *New York Times* article "Wayward Christian Soldiers," which emerged from the book you were completing at the time. One thing you note in that article is that the power that evangelicals have amassed in the last decade has compromised our witness and our message and that our drive for access and power has been what you call a Faustian bargain; I was wondering if you could give our readers a brief genealogy of that bargain and how it is playing out in our culture.

Charles Marsh (**CM**): I think that, certainly, we have seen over the past several decades presidents courting the evangelical community. But I have not seen anything like the veritable marriage of the Republican Party and white evangelicalism that we've observed in the first six years of the Bush administration, and I try to talk about the historical origins of that Faustian bargain in the book, *Wayward Christian Soldiers*. There are a variety of reasons; I would say that at the very heart of this marriage is a theological mistake, and it's one that is very familiar. I mean, Karl Barth, in thinking about the dead end of the Protestant Liberal establishment in Germany in the early part of the twentieth century, talked about a tradition that had started to speak of God, or grown accustomed to speaking of God, by speaking of humanity in a loud voice. I think that despite all of our self-righteous talk and our very loud piety we've grown accustomed to speaking of God by speaking of our own preferences, ambitions, and values in a loud voice. So there are profound theological mistakes at play in our confusion of patriotism and discipleship as well as in our seeming willingness to allow the language of the gospel to be used as partisan talking points.

You know, certainly evangelicals—and I grew up in an evangelical community, my father is a Southern Baptist minister, I was educated in an evangelical college prior to going to graduate school—I think some of us grew impatient on the margins of power, and so this opportunity to move from the margins to the corridors of political power proved too great to resist. We offered our blessings on this marriage between conservative politics and white evangelicalism—and was it not a marriage that benefited hugely the conservative evangelical politicos? But as you noted in your question, it is also [a marriage] that has inevitably led to the profanation of the gospel in our time, [to] the cheapening of the proclamation. That's one way I would begin talking about it.

TOJ: I think one thing that would be good to name for the readers is, specifically, when you say that evangelicals have compromised the witness and the message with this joining of power, what do you think is the biggest part of that witness and message that has been compromised?

CM: Well, I mean let's look for example at the war sermons preached by evangelicals in the fall of 2002 and the spring of 2003. One of the most depressing exercises I've ever undertaken is sitting at my desk looking at the dozens of sermons preached to evangelical congregations that had the effect of rallying the laity to [nearly] unanimous support of the invasion of Iraq, 87 percent of white evangelicals according to a Pew poll. You asked what was most cheapened; well, one of the things that I discovered in the sermons was that Jesus made only a rare appearance and even then he appeared more as a pain in the ass than the Lord of all creation, you know, someone who spoiled all the fun in our national military ambitions—which of course he did! So Jesus appears [in these sermons] only to be quickly ushered out the door as soon as possible. Much more attention in the war sermons is given to esoteric passages in First and Second Kings—or a nod or two in the direction of the Just War doctrine, but that doesn't work because of the criterion of last resort. In the end, one hears a kind of hallowing acquiescence to President George W. Bush's authority to mediate God's will to the nation. There is a perception that he is a brother in Christ, and he discerns the will of the nation, that we are to go to Iraq, and that he gets these messages directly from his Heavenly Father. Never mind scripture and tradition and all those aggravating moral rules we are obliged to practice as people baptized into the Body of Christ. Our president has an immediate relationship to the divine, and we will comply with his will by any means necessary. You have ministers like Charles Stanley, who are saying in their sermons that churches must accommodate the war by whatever means necessary.

In the end, not only are scripture, tradition, and the global ecumenical church marginalized, but the sermons give voice to a Christian piety without discipleship, which is to say, a piety without Jesus.

TOJ: A piety that seems to play out in a kind of foreign policy that, like you said, has nothing to do with Jesus.

CM: That's right. It is a foreign policy that is baptized in all the jingoistic fervor of American values and American patriotism. There is a profound confusion between loyalty to nation and loyalty to the Christian tradition. And that is the anatomy of idolatry, isn't it?

TOJ: If this is the case for us, what would you say the evangelical community needs to do to rescind this bargain that we've made?

CM: First of all, I want to say that I am speaking as an evangelical Christian. I wrote this book in a couple of stages. The first draft, with its numerous revisions, was written before the midterm elections of 2006. The midterms changed the whole landscape of religion and politics, and so the manuscript needed to be recast. I wrote the book initially as a jeremiad. I was angry, as many of us were angry, with all the insanity, and the book included more (by now) familiar criticisms of the Christian Right. But after the midterm elections, it seemed to me that some important new notes were being heard, particularly among the evangelical laity, and I took a few months to perform some deep surgery on the book, looking critically at my authorial tone, and to make more clear the fact that I'm really speaking as an evangelical and someone who is complicit in this.

Although I do offer some very direct criticisms of evangelical church leaders, my purpose became more of [a response] to the question "Where do we go from here?" That seemed to me a question that was beginning to be heard after the midterm elections—not just as a result of the loss of political power but out of a sense of theological mistakes made. I continue to hear these sentiments among the laity but not among the leaders. The conservative elites still seem unapologetic. Charles Colson wrote an article in the *Washington Post* a couple of weeks ago in which he tried to make the case that the continued occupation of Iraq fulfills Just War criteria—a real extraordinary feat. I didn't hear a sense of, "we have made mistakes, and so what do we do now?" or any concern with the undeniable fact that the "cause of Christ," as we used to say in the churches, had been hurt severely by our political behavior.

I mean, can *Christianity Today* not take some time to ask how we shall then live after this period of compromise, of accommodation, of theological mistakes so great [that] they have aided in the unleashing of enormous violent forces in the world? I think that's where I really wanted to move in the final revisions of the book, and obviously the first step was a willingness to think honestly about the damage done and a willingness to engage in serious soul-searching and a penitent heart, to be quiet before the Lord with a repentant and truthful heart. When I appeal to the discipline of silence in the book, this is not some media ploy or a sensationalistic call to shut up. John Wilson in *Books and Culture*, who attacked my book in a July review, though without any engagement with the theological substance of the book, titled his piece, "Be Silent—and Buy My Book." Surely he is aware of the time-honored practice in the Christian tradition of being quiet before the Lord. Dietrich Bonhoeffer spoke of a silence that brings "purification, clarification, and concentration upon the essential thing." Can evangelical Christians in America seriously deny that churches desperately need this kind of discipline? So I wrote about a time of confession, a remembering of who we are, of having the humility to say that we have made grave mistakes, mistakes with far-reaching global consequences. And we must humbly stand in God's presence and seek forgiveness.

In my wildest dreams, I sometimes imagine that one of Billy Graham's final calls to revival and renewal will be a convening in Washington—on the same mall where Dr. King shared with us his dream—a gathering of hundreds of thousands, maybe millions, of evangelicals in repentance for the church's support of the devastation of Iraq. I think in smaller groups and individual devotionals and churches, Christian colleges, magazines, and institutions, we all need to be thinking seriously about what repentance looks like.

TOJ: It is interesting that you went in that direction, because in this issue, *TOJ* is talking about both individual and corporate psychopathology; we are focusing on the way sins form our psyches. In doing this, and I think we've been good about it so far, we are trying to name the malformations that evangelicals have fallen into.

CM: Well, there are a lot more. If you've read the book, you know. This whole kind of messianic impulse that drives so many of us in the evangelical world, which I've noted and you've certainly noted too, I have been thinking about for a long time. My three books that preceded *Wayward Christian Soldiers* all treated in some degree the culture of Southern evangelicalism in the 1960s. The current situation seems too familiar, like a Southern-evangelical-segregationist-Gnostic heresy writ large. You know, good Lord, I thought I'd gotten away from that, and now we're all that way!

TOJ: You mention silence and repentance as possible ways out, but I wonder if you'd speak about more? While focusing on sins, what we're also trying to do in this issue of *TOJ* is to talk about virtues that lead toward healing. With this notion of a conflation of flag and cross that kind of dominates the Gospel—and I would include myself in this category, evangelicalism is where I'm coming from as well—what are some virtues or practices of discipline that we can inculcate to pull apart the tentacles of flag and cross that we have allowed to intertwine so completely?

CM: We are living in a critical period of time, and one wonders whether it may not be now appropriate to call it a day on the American evangelical project. Nonetheless, in this time, if we have any hope of moving forward, we must reaffirm the Christian faith's essential affirmations and seek to live in simple devotion to Jesus. What are these essential affirmations? Practicing hospitality to strangers; affirming the sacred character of all created life; learning how to engage the world as healers and participants rather than as manipulators or as people who control the script; learning to be still in God's presence; keeping the mysteries of the faith from profanation; [and] remembering our citizenship in the global, ecumenical Body of Christ [by] living as builders of just and human community [and] working, as Dr. King admonished in his extraordinary sermon [at] the end of the 1956 Montgomery Bus Boycott, [toward] redemption, reconciliation, and the creation of beloved community. Learning to be peculiar rather than to be relevant. We must remember that God is fully God without America. It is really learning all over again what it means to say yes to the call of Jesus and what it means to take that first step.

Bonhoeffer in the *Cost of Discipleship* said that the first step changes everything, that acts of obedience are a step into a new world. Discipleship means learning to practice the citizenship of this new world in the world that we are all in.

TOJ: Well, I was going to ask you in one of the later questions, but I guess I'll ask you now. Your earlier work (and I guess you continue to work on him in some of the pieces you've written that I have seen) was on Bonhoeffer, and you know the context of Bonhoeffer was vastly different than our present context and yet there are also many things that are somewhat similar—military hostilities, domestic oppression, and persecution of certain people groups—and one of the points that you have made is that Bonhoeffer was not just a pastor but a theologian working through some of these issues and even a philosopher. My question is, how do you as a professor of religion and an evangelical see yourself as struggling with this mixture of the public/private that is written so deeply into our culture? How do you find yourself wrestling with that and working off of Bonhoeffer to do that?

CM: Yeah, that's a great question. I have been mindful time and again of one of the letters from Tegel Prison to [Eberhard] Bethge, when Bonhoeffer writes that the time of words is over. Our witness must now be limited to two things: prayer and righteous action. Bonhoeffer had a sense that the language of the gospel, its ability to speak to the world with power and freshness, and not just to communicate but to instantiate the reconciling love of God, had been obliterated in its misuse, by its misuse. He imagined a certain kind of necessity in righteous action and prayer. You might remember, too, in a passage in *Ethics* there is a similarly mind-boggling passage. I would love to convene a symposium of theologians and pastors around this one paragraph. Bonhoeffer says, "In earlier times the church could preach that a person must first become a sinner, like the publican and the harlot, before he could know and find Christ, but we in our time must say rather that before a person can know and find Christ he must first become righteous like those who strive and who suffer for the sake of justice, truth and humanity." I mean, that is an extraordinary remark that speaks to us in this moment.

The way that I try to negotiate the private and public right now is by recognizing that this is a time when evangelical Christians, and all Christians, must learn what it means to affirm humanity. Many of us, in all of our post-liberal zeal to retrieve Christian particularity, have spent a lot of time emphasizing our linguistic, contextual uniqueness, our own peculiar sort of logic, the special sense of our distinctive truth claims—and I'm not at all suggesting that Christians relinquish the particularity of the gospel or the specificity of the gospel, not at all—but one of the forms that repentance might take is a renewed commitment to humanity and a humility that leads to a greater service of the world. We might begin to live out our particularity in service to humanity.

TOJ: That seems to me a very interesting concept. Then, at the end of the age of the humanist, Christianity was defining itself against that kind of ideology, and now, at the end of the age of the secular humanist, it might be Christianity's challenge to proclaim the humanity of people.

CM: Lovely. You know Barth said somewhere in the *Word of God and the Word of Man*, "we must be more romantic than the romantics, more humanist than the humanists, but we must be more precise . . ." and honestly, more precise might be the most important part of that admonition. I think that that precision has often been claimed as a possession that we wield over others rather than as a gift that really enables genuine community. Why not think of Christian discipleship as a journey to authentic humanism?

We [The Program on Lived Theology, University of Virginia] have John de Gruchy, a South African theologian, coming to speak on his new book, *Confessions of a Christian Humanist*. And yes, it seems like an important theme at the moment. I can't say that it is an important theme for the church in Latin America or the church in Europe—I don't know—but I think that in our context, and particularly in light of the contempt for the global, ecumenical church, displayed by both evangelicals and liberals in the United States, this theological theme speaks to us with a kind of urgency.

TOJ: Dr. Marsh, please let me ask one final question. Given that this is what some people are referring to as a post-civil rights era, how do we begin to work toward, or how do we see, reconciliation in this time? What does it look like? What language do we use to talk about this very important idea of reconciliation and opening ourselves in hospitality to other people? So taking what we've learned from civil rights and the shortcomings we've learned from the civil rights movement, how do we go forward?

CM: My dear friend, the civil-rights saint and Student Nonviolent Coordinating Committee (SNCC) field secretary, Victoria Gray Adams, who passed away last winter of a brain tumor, was a church woman and a business leader in Hattiesburg, Mississippi, who became a field secretary for the SNCC and a sister-traveler with Fannie Lou Hamer, an extraordinary woman of faith. I was privileged to get to know Ms. Adams and to work with her in the Project on Lived Theology over the past seven years. She lived in Petersburg, Virginia, and served as the Wesleyan chaplain at Virginia State University. The last time she visited with me she was speaking to my Bonhoeffer-King seminar in my home. It was a winter afternoon; we had a fire going, and there was just a wonderful spirit in the room. She was a riveting storyteller. She had us singing and praying; and she had a gift of invoking the spirit of the Movement in a way that was palpable. I am so sorry that she is gone, although I am moved by the thought that Ms. Gray and Ms. Hamer are breaking bread together in heaven. In what proved to be our last conversation, Ms. Adams was asked by a student about the mission of the civil rights movement today. Without hesitation she said, "It is learning to speak the language of peace." And I think she put her finger precisely on the need, the *kairos*, of our situation. I certainly think that the practice of peace and learning to speak the language of peace includes a variety of attendant practices, but her answer would be the first response I would give to your question.

TOJ: Given the scenario that we find ourselves in, it is amazing to me how much evangelicals have a dearth of the language of peace. Within a survey of evangelical sermons I would think that peace is something that pops up either infrequently or not at all. So there is a deep need to regain that as a theological concept, and not as a concept but as a practice, a lived practice that is deeply important to us.

CM: Absolutely. Let's hope that this exchange helps usher in a renewal of this language.

chapter 8

Why Everything
Must Change

An Interview with Brian McLaren

by Jon Stanley

ISSUE #10 OF *The Other Journal* focused on virtue, sin, and psychopathology in the new millennium. Our discussion of these topics was launched by an interview with Brian McLaren, a leading voice in the emerging church movement and author of the recently released *Everything Must Change: Jesus, Global Crises, and a Revolution of Hope*. In the interview, McLaren speaks candidly about the deep pathology that is driving civilization into environmental, economic, and security crises and about the ways in which Western Christianity is complicit in these calamities. McLaren also moves beyond a cultural diagnosis and offers substantive proposals for positive change. We talked with McLaren about why everything must change and what Jesus might have to say about the kinds of change that are needed.

The Other Journal (*TOJ*): You describe your book, *Everything Must Change: Jesus, Global Crises, and a Revolution of Hope*, as growing out of and revolving around two preoccupying questions. What are these questions?

Brian McLaren (**BM**): Back in my twenties I remember asking a question that has stayed with me ever since then: what are the most serious crises facing our world? That question has been with me for a long time. And then a second question naturally follows: what does Jesus have to say to those top global crises?

TOJ: In your book you describe these as very live, timely, and personal questions prompted by current life experiences and political realities and as building upon themes you've taken up in your previous writing (particularly in *The Secret Message of Jesus*), yet also as questions that every person serious about faith or ethics must eventually take to heart. So how did these questions come to the fore for you at this particular point in your life and theological journey, and why are they important for everyone to consider?

BM: Let me start by way of my own story, my own narrative. In the late eighties and early nineties, I would have considered myself a well-educated conservative evangelical. I was always on the innovative side of things, but I wouldn't have really rocked the boat on many issues.

TOJ: That's kind of hard to believe [*smile*]. It would be very interesting to have known you then.

BM: I mean, I came from the Jesus movement, so in many ways I've seen the really good side of evangelicalism, and I had a lot of great experiences. So that's my background. But in the early nineties, in large part because my main calling is evangelism, I was really listening to the questions that people were asking me. By the way, this is one of the ways the seeker-sensitive movement has really had a far-reaching impact. I know many people are critical about a lot of things related to the seeker movement, but I think this particular influence is very profound and very positive. When you say, as Bill Hybels says, "Lost people matter to God," then they start to matter to you, and then you start to listen to their questions; you don't just dismiss them as unsaved or whatever. Well, their questions re-opened for me something I had encountered a long time ago in graduate school, and that's postmodern philosophy, and this cultural shift from a modern to a postmodern culture. So in the early nineties I started grappling with that shift, and it really was tough. Then in the late nineties, I started writing about it because I started to feel a little bit of hope.

TOJ: Would that have been your book, *A New Kind of Christian*?

BM: That's right, my first book where I opened this up was *Church on the Other Side*, and then in the *New Kind of Christian* series I opened it up some more. If you want to use a term that comes out of that postmodern world, the word would be *deconstruction*. I was undergoing a deconstruction. Not a deconstruction of my faith as a personal trust in God, but of my theological categories and of my theological methodology. So that's not an easy thing to go through, but once you do a lot of deconstruction, then you have to start reconstructing or else you end up with nothing but a bunch of fragments. And for me that reconstruction drove me, or drew me, back to the Gospels. And so the last several years I have been spending huge amounts of my spiritual attention on trying to understand Jesus again and trying to read the Bible with as much of a second naïveté as I possibly can. And that resulted in my previous book, *The Secret Message of Jesus*.

Well, one of the things that hit me in that exploration in a really profound way is that to understand Jesus you have to understand his time, particularly the first-century context. You know, we would think it's ridiculous to try to understand Martin Luther King Jr. or Abraham Lincoln without knowing something about the history of slavery, the Civil War, and civil rights in America. Well, very often we do just that with Jesus, abstracting him from his situation in order to try to understand him. And so the last several years I've been trying to understand Jesus in his own context. N. T. Wright challenges you to this.

TOJ: Yeah, I am curious who your guides were in this new reading of Jesus in his first-century context.

BM: N. T. Wright's work has been really, really influential in my thinking. And then people like Dominic Crossan. I think Dominic is doing some great work on this front. And Marcus Borg as well, even though I think a lot people really misunderstand him. All of them are saying: we feel there is more to Jesus than what is often given credit! And then there are people like Richard Horsley and Ched Myers writing on the relationship between Jesus and the Roman Empire. And of course, the Latin American liberation theologians have a lot of insight into Jesus and his context. For example, John Sobrino's *Jesus the Liberator* and Leonardo Boff's *Jesus Christ Liberator*; these were really phenomenal books for me. So I was reading everything I could get my hands on about Jesus from a variety of perspectives. Not rejecting my evangelical understanding of Jesus at all, but not believing it had given me the whole story. So when you realize that Jesus was addressing a lot of the most pressing questions and issues in his own day, then you can't help but ask what Jesus has to say about the most pressing questions and issues in ours.

TOJ: One of the things you've done throughout your writing, and perhaps most explicitly in *Everything Must Change*, is that you've introduced your readers to thinkers and writers that have been meaningful to you in your journey and who your largely evangelical readership might not otherwise encounter. This has actually been a point of criticism from some in more conservative circles. I recall reading one particular interview where your interlocutor said something to the effect of, "That sounds like liberation theology; you're not reading them are you?" How would you make a case for the value of broadening our theological exposure and expanding our dialogue partners as evangelicals?

BM: Well, the first thing I would want to say is that I would read one paragraph of N. T. Wright or listen to one CD of a lecture he gave at Regent Seminary in Vancouver and then go back and read the New Testament. What was exciting wasn't N. T. Wright—no insult to N. T. Wright; I hope people say the same thing about my books. What was exciting were the Gospels themselves. I'd go back and read Matthew and Luke, and that was the stuff that was really transformative. So mentioning different lists of names isn't that important, but what's really important is that this stuff has been simmering in the biblical text itself, and we've been very well-trained not to see it. We've been trained to look for certain things and not for others. One of my mentors has a great statement: "What you focus on determines what you miss." So we go to the Bible being very well-trained to focus on certain things, and we miss all the other things. That's a huge theme of *Everything Must Change*, and I really hope it will help people who love the Bible and love Jesus to notice things that have been there all along but that we have been trained not to see.

TOJ: When you speak of your book growing out of the experience of reading contemporary crisis literature together with the Gospels in their first-century context, I couldn't help thinking of a particular statement by Karl Barth: "Christians must read the world with the newspaper in one hand and the Bible in the other." Is such *double-reading* a conscious methodology for you?

BM: You know, I imagine I always would have agreed with Karl Barth on that, and I think I probably understand a little bit more of what he meant now. For example, I've heard very fundamentalist pastors quote that, and they don't mention Barth's name, of course. But what they mean is to look for anecdotes from contemporary culture that you can bring in while teaching the Bible. And I guess that's a good start. It's better than being in this hermetically sealed religious ghetto. But I think part of what Barth was saying is that the headlines of the newspaper tell us what the crises are, and that God is very concerned about the crises of our world, and when you are touched by those crises and you open the pages of the Bible, you begin to notice things that you wouldn't notice otherwise.

So when you read in the newspaper about the serious gap between the world's rich and the world's poor, and that the gap is expanding—the rich are getting richer at a phenomenally fast rate, and the poor are staying about the same or at best getting only a tiny bit better—well, then you go to the Bible and read the story about the rich man and Lazarus. And see, we're trained to think that this is a story about who goes to heaven and who goes to hell. By the way, even in this way of reading, it doesn't turn out the way many of our traditional theologies would lead us to expect. But then you realize that this is really a story that tells us that God cares deeply about poor people and calls us to care deeply as well.

TOJ: That's very helpful as an example of the way such double-reading—reading the Bible in light of the world and reading the world in light of the Bible—calls us to address what you describe in your books as the *equity crisis*. Your book is full of this kind of work, showing how an understanding of today's world can actually help us be better readers of the Bible.

BM: I hope so! I hope people will feel that this is really a book—maybe more so than any other of my books—about reading the Bible. But the opposite is also true. If you read the Bible, you begin to notice certain themes, and that enables you to see certain things that others might miss when you read the headlines. For example, the headlines in the United States especially are filled with things like "U.S. versus Islamic Fundamentalists," and so that's the narrative we're given. But you see, when you read the Bible you begin to see that evil—and Calvin highlighted this in his doctrine of total depravity—doesn't reside on one side or the other, but that it resides on both sides. So when I hear our president making it sound like we are virtuous and "they" are evil, my reading of the Bible makes me suspicious of my president. So to me, this is the way it should be, God wants us to be readers and thinkers of the Bible, and we must do that in the world, but not be of it.

TOJ: So our president, who confesses to be a Bible-believing Christian, isn't employing a very biblical understanding of evil. And to be fair, it's not only our president who has a simplistic understanding of evil—the idea that we can locate evil here or there is pervasive.

BM: Exactly, the us/them approach to evil is far more simplistic than what we find in the scriptures. This is where a biblical understanding of evil can really speak into the mutual demonization that is escalating into what I refer to as the security crisis.

TOJ: You refer to *Everything Must Change* as your most worldly book to date, in that you take the world and its contemporary social, political, ecological, and economic realities as a subject of rigorous analysis. One doesn't find many books of this sort in the average evangelical bookstore. Why don't we see more worldly books? And how do the type of books one is likely to find (self-help, end-times, et cetera) reveal the ethos of evangelicalism and what evangelical priorities are?

BM: It would really be a very interesting study to go in and look at all the new book releases in a six month period in the Christian book-publishing world and even to do the same for the subjects of Christian radio broadcasts and television and then to make assessments on what's really important to us based on what we find. And I wouldn't criticize those things; people read those books because that's what's important to them and they find them helpful. But here's the problem: let's say I want to read a prosperity-gospel book about how to pray in order to get rich. Now, if global warming is even partially true, and if we are pushing our environment beyond its limits of sustainability, then we are going to eventually reach a point where the environment is so degraded that nobody's prayers for prosperity are ever going to get answered. In so doing we lean on one part of the biblical text—verses about prayer and the promises of God—and we completely forget about another part of the biblical text that speaks about wisdom, foresight, responsibility, and stewardship. And this is the great danger, you see: we say we are biblical, but we get a choice about which things we emphasize.

TOJ: Even here, as you're critiquing the prosperity-gospel movement as being misguided, you're quick to acknowledge the part of the Bible they are rightly tapping into. This spirit of appreciative critique seems to characterize your work.

BM: If I could maybe make a little side comment about that. I appreciate you noticing that, because one of the few terribly ugly things that's going on in the evangelical world, the Islamic world, and all throughout the political world, really—and this goes back to our discussion about a biblical understanding of evil and how it can help us to effectively address the complexity of the security crisis—is the vilification of those with whom we disagree. To vilify and demonize people with whom we disagree sets all sorts of terrible things in motion. I think this is why Jesus says in the Sermon on the Mount not to call your brother an idiot and that you're liable for judgment if you do so. He says to love your enemies and to do good to people who do evil to you, which stops so many terrible things from getting set in motion.

If I call anyone with whom I disagree a heretic, infidel, idiot, or whatever, it is a way of excluding them. Or even calling someone insane, which is politically a very powerful word, you know, we simply say, "the terrorists are insane." Or even a word like *evil*. Evil almost removes from us the obligation to understand them, you know: "there's nothing to understand; they're just evil." By using words like that we've stopped listening and we've dehumanized the other, making it possible to treat them in horrible ways. So Jesus says, take all the people in that category and love them, and that is what truly brings transformation. Demonization is a huge problem in our debates on these issues.

TOJ: In a previous *TOJ* interview with Miroslav Volf, professor Volf stressed the point that "the task set before the theologian is that of addressing the great issues of the day from a theological point of view," a task you have explicitly taken up in this book. One can see this world-formative orientation in the work of many theologians around the world (take Jürgen Moltmann, for example, who has analyzed and commented upon nearly every significant social and political issue in the latter half of the twentieth century), yet as a whole it doesn't seem to characterize the tenor of evangelical theology in North America. Why is it that North American evangelical theologians tend to focus on issues of method and doctrine rather than, as Volf says, on "the great issues of the day"?

BM: Well, we have to remember that evangelical identity is very complex and that it changes over time. And the terms *evangelical* and *fundamentalist* are very slippery, and it's hard to tell where one starts and the other stops. And the proportion of the people who are evangelicals—whom we call fundamentalists—rises and falls over the decades.

TOJ: Fair enough. I am presuming a lot when I speak of evangelicals as a whole.

BM: These terms are all so slippery for all of us. For example, in the nineteenth century, there were people we would call evangelicals, people passionate about their faith and personal relationship with Christ, devoted in prayer, believing in Jesus as their savior, and desiring to share their faith—all great markers of evangelicalism. Well, these evangelicals were the leaders in the feminist movement, and (a lot of people don't know this) the animal rights movement was really born out of evangelical fervor. And of course, the abolition movement, although to be honest, evangelicals probably defended slavery in far greater numbers than opposed it. But there certainly were evangelicals at the forefront of opposing it as well.

And so, you know, we have a complex history. But right now, it seems what's happened in the last few decades is that, because of the Religious Right, evangelical forays into public life have been focused on what some people call pelvic issues or genital issues or sexual issues. So evangelicals have been focused on abortion and homosexual marriage, and I do think those issues are important—in the book I have a section where I talk a little bit about abortion—but the issue to me is by being preoccupied with those issues, we've effectively missed the larger issues that I think actually fuel some of the symptoms. In this sense, we've dealt with the symptoms and not the causes.

But if you want to talk about evangelicals who really have affirmed the need for evangelicals to be involved in public life in a positive way, then people like Jim Wallis, Tony Campolo, and Ron Sider come to mind right away. But I think we also have to pay attention to people from Latin

America like René Padilla and Samuel Escobar. There have been many, many people who have done this well in my opinion, but a lot of them are non-white and non-American, and so, sadly, they haven't been heard. But you know, John Stott would be a great example of an English evangelical deeply concerned about a wide range of social issues.

TOJ: Yes, you quote Stott extensively in your book.

BM: I do, and I think many people don't appreciate the fact that John has been reflecting on these issues for decades and has a lot of very wise things to say. Not only because of the length of time he's been reflecting on these issues, but also because of his decades-long friendship with René Padilla from Latin America.

TOJ: Now I wouldn't say this with respect to the security crisis per se, but on the whole, the evangelical community seems very resistant to the thesis that the world really is suffering from an equity crisis and an environmental crisis. If this is accurate, why do you think this is so? Is it political, out of the refusal to believe anything Al Gore and the Hollywood liberals have to say? Is it theological, in that reigning evangelical views of Providence or sovereignty relegate world crises to a theological impossibility? Or is it more pragmatic—that admitting to crisis implies, as you say, that everything must change, which would require a radical reorientation of the American way of life?

BM: First of all, I think that's a very important question, and part of me doesn't want to give an answer just because I think it deserves a lot of reflection. But I'll offer a couple of thoughts. First, not just as evangelicals, but as Western Christians, we have a leaning toward emphasizing personal sin and minimizing social sin. We tend to focus on personal righteousness rather than social justice, but the Bible doesn't make that distinction. Now in the Catholic church there is a deep tradition of Catholic social teaching, but on the popular level, largely because of the abortion issue, even many Roman Catholics are now focused almost exclusively on personal morality. When they hear the word *morality* they immediately think sex. But biblical justice and biblical righteousness is inherently integral; it brings together both the social and the personal. So that would be one problem.

A second problem—a huge problem—is our eschatology. The dominance of *Left Behind* eschatology means that millions of American

Christians expect the world to get worse, believe it's God's will for the world to get worse, and that the worse it gets, the happier they feel they should be because it means they will get raptured all the sooner. I think this is a gross misreading of the biblical text. I think three hundred years from now people will look back on this reading of the text like the way we look at people who believed the world was flat or that the sun rotated around the earth. However, it's very popular right now.

And the third problem is political. Because of the Religious Right in recent decades, the issues of abortion and homosexuality have been used to gain percentage points in elections for one party and against another party. And that has led some powerful evangelical leaders to say: "We can't talk about the environment because that will dilute attention from our high-leverage issues."

TOJ: The therapeutic world has been telling us for years that in order for things to get better in the future, we must first acknowledge how bad things are in the present. You seem to employ this therapeutic wisdom (which also happens to be very biblical) in both your book and in your *Deep Shift* material that is meant as a follow-up to the book.[1] A friend and I were perusing your *Deep Shift* website, and he read the phrase "We are in Deep Shift" as saying "We are in Deep Shit." Before he realized what it really said, his response was that of relief, saying, "Finally, someone's willing to acknowledge the shit we are in." Now, I don't know if you intended this textual echo, but as you've been communicating this crisis material over the past few months, has the response been more characterized by relief, like my friend, or by resistance?

BM: Well, it's interesting how it ends up being very polarizing. I don't want to be polarizing, but what tends to happen is that some people are saying, "Everything has changed too much already. We've got to get back to keep things the same as they were in the past." So those people don't like to hear this stuff—it's uncomfortable for them. But I think there are a lot of people, and I'm finding this as I interact with people, who say, "Ah, finally somebody is giving us a chance to bring into the light of day our anxiety about the direction we're going." There's a theological dimension to that anxiety, but it's also economic, political, military, and social.

---

1. See *DeepShift* at http://deepshift.org.

In the book, I tell a story about being in East Africa with a lot of Rwandans who look back on the Rwandan genocide of 1994, one of the most horrific genocides in history, which took place among people who all go to church—almost all of them go to church. And in fact, it was the Muslims who actually participated in the genocide less than the Christians. So there is something in them that says, "Something is wrong with the way we're doing this." And it has given them the space to admit, "You know, it's shameful to have to face what we did, but let's go into the shame and try to understand what's really going on here." To me, this is the kind of thing that has to happen if there is to be real change.

TOJ: It's been said that only those with great hope can generate the courage to face how bad things really are, whether that be in our personal lives, our relationships, or in our world. So in many ways, your book is communicating not only a message of crises but also a message of hope.

BM: My friend Jim Wallis says this, from his experience of speaking all over the country: "The real choice we have to make is between hope on the one hand and cynicism, despair, and resignation on the other." I really feel that.

TOJ: How did you come to identify these particular crises—prosperity, security, equity, and spirituality—as the key crises in our time?

BM: As I said, I knew I wanted to address this question about global crises, but I had no idea what books were out there, so I did like anybody would do—I started on the internet. I started googling "global crisis," "global problems," et cetera. And it doesn't take too long, you know. Five or six hours on the internet, and you've covered hundreds of people talking about this and that and maybe twenty books or so. And so I started on the internet, then I just started reading books. And I was so happy there were some books, but I was quite surprised to find out how few books there are out there that are really looking at crises globally. But I think this is starting to happen more and more. It's happening among economists, biologists, political scientists, and theologians.

Then the challenge was to look at all these different lists and to try to figure out how to integrate these—how they relate. Literally, I spent months with a couple of yellow pads with notes and diagrams and lists and compiled lists, and I just fooled around with it until I began feeling some stuff click into place. And you know, it ends up being quite simple, but it's usually a complicated process getting to simplicity.

TOJ: One of the strongest theses in your book is the idea that these crises are in fact interrelated and driven by a common social pathology. I suppose this is why, if anything is to really change, everything must change.

BM: Yeah. As I started trying to work with these lists, it really became very clear to me that these issues were interrelated. The first thing you realize is that there are all these lists, and an effect in one list is a cause in another list, you know, and you see the complexity of this, and you begin to realize that you cannot deal with these as discrete items.

For example, you can say that malaria is a terrible problem in Africa, and that it's an easy problem to solve because we can solve it with mosquito nets and other things. But then the question is, well, why haven't they acquired mosquito nets already? Well, then you have to deal with economic issues. And then you realize that if we solve the malaria problem in the next few years, and we go on to the next problem and ask why we haven't solved it yet, well, once again there is an economic problem behind it.

So you find yourself drawn to economics, because that's the way in which a lot of these issues are related. It goes back a little bit to that election slogan in the nineties, "It's the economy, stupid," but I think it's true in a far deeper way than people realize. So a group of the problems cluster around issues of economics as they relate first to the environment and second to redistribution and opportunity.

So those are my first two crises: the prosperity crisis and the equity crisis. And then there are a whole group of them that flow out of the fact that you have a lot of people desperately poor and other people extravagantly rich in a world that is under increasing stress because of environmental changes in a civilization that doesn't have much of a margin for environmental change. You put those things together, and then you have a security crisis. So I saw those three things—prosperity, equity, and security—as really being interwoven.

But then the question that I asked myself was "Why aren't we solving those problems?" And that's where this idea of *framing stories* came in. And that, to me, is the fourth crisis, and in some ways it's like the drive shaft that drives the three first crises. If we have a dysfunctional framing story, then it either makes us respond to the first three crises in counter-productive ways, or it simply makes us oblivious to them.

Let me use an example from the family. Say you have a man who's really a lousy husband and a terrible father, and he's driven by the story in his mind—the framing story—that the solution to all family problems is to be a strong authoritarian father. So whenever his wife or children complain, his solution is, "I've got to be tougher. I've got to be tougher." The more he lives by that framing story, the more he destroys his family, even though his desire is to have a good family and to be a good father. And that's the kind of thing I'm looking at in terms of culture and civilization: what are those kinds of stories at work in our corporate soul?

TOJ: That example demonstrates a way of working with the relationship between desire and framing story that's very interesting. It seems that it allows you to honor good desire even when the operative framing story is bending it in a particularly destructive direction.

BM: It's interesting that the understanding of desire really becomes key in this, because the desire for prosperity, equity, and security are all good desires. And this may bring us back to Saint Thomas Aquinas who said that "the essence of evil is the corruption of a good desire." So a good framing story can harness those desires toward holiness, goodness, and justice, but a bad framing story can harness those desires toward oppression and destruction.

TOJ: Speaking of the relatedness of particular crises, as I was reading your book, I was also reading Georg Hegel's *Elements of the Philosophy of Right*, in which he argues that a state where individuals are free to pursue their economic self-interest in an unlimited manner will inevitably become characterized by radical economic inequity and social unrest and thus will necessarily become a police state. That sounds so much like your analysis of the relationship between the prosperity crisis, equity crisis, and security crisis on the global level. And I thought to myself, either you've read Hegel, or you are both onto a deep insight into the nature of society.

BM: You know, I've never read that in Hegel, but to me this is really exciting, because of course I don't think my book is the final word to solve all the problems. But if my book can help other people like you notice things elsewhere, and then patterns begin to emerge among different writers that lead us forward, then see, that brings the conversation forward. So it's very encouraging to me to hear that.

TOJ: By the way, your analysis was written much more accessibly than Hegel's [*laughter*]. But I'd say that's characteristic of the book as a whole as well. You've taken the crisis literature, which is typically written for other academics, and really made it accessible to those of us who are unfamiliar with the professional lingo.

BM: Well, thanks. I do hope I've done that in the book. And you know, much of the literature is becoming more accessible to the interested reader. There are a whole bunch of economists who are coming to understand that economics is so important that they realize they actually have to learn to speak plain English [*laughter*]. And that's a trend that I expect will continue.

TOJ: When you speak about the contemporary global situation, you do so in terms of a *suicide machine*. How does this metaphor draw things together for you?

BM: Well, when you think about civilization, in many ways it's like a machine. It's this complex structure that we put together to help us achieve these three good desires for prosperity, equity, and security. Not to say there aren't other desires too, but those seem to be the fundamental purposes of civilization. But if that machine is driven by bad programming, and once again, the term I use for this is a *destructive framing story*, then the very machinery that you've built to help you becomes machinery that can destroy you. That's why I call it a suicide machine. And you know, it's interesting that this shows up in modern film. You think about a movie like *The Matrix*. It's about a machine that we've built turning on us. Or the movie *I, Robot*. Or even the movie *Titanic,* in a certain way. It's a machine that we've put our confidence into to take us where we want to go, and because of the hubris or overconfidence that drives it, we sink!

TOJ: This critique of human overconfidence is a strong theme in your book.

BM: You know, in a way, this brings us back to really core issues as Christians, and especially as evangelicals, because we believe that we are saved by faith. And the issue is, do we have faith in God and in God's ways, or do we have faith in our own techniques? And I think Jesus's call to us to have faith in him is a call to stop trusting in these external systems. In his day it was "Stop trusting the gospel of Caesar" or "Stop trusting the gospel of the Zealots who think they can beat Caesar by using Caesar's methods," and "I'm offering a different gospel (or news), in fact, *good news* to trust in."

TOJ: That's a very earthy and refreshing interpretation of salvation by faith, which is commonly taken to refer solely to how one gets to heaven after they die.

BM: Yeah, you know, in Romans 1 when Paul writes, "The just shall live by faith," he's actually quoting Habakkuk. And when Habakkuk is writing, he's not writing about how you get to heaven. He's saying, you know, we're about to be conquered by the expanding empire next door, and the only way to survive this security crisis is not to trust in an arms race of horses and chariots but through faith in God, which means being faithful and just before God.

TOJ: You are openly critical of a simplistic What Would Jesus Do (WWJD) approach to global crises. Yet you maintain that a serious study of Jesus and his proclamation that "the kingdom is at hand" can give us invaluable insight and direction in engaging the most serious problems in our world. How so?

BM: Well, yes, one of the things I definitely want to avoid is the simplistic WWJD thing. It's really the urge of fundamentalism to want to take things from ancient texts and assume we'll solve today's problems if we simply slap the texts onto contemporary situations. That's part of what Sharia law is about, and I think it's part of a reactionary tendency among some Christians. I think they're almost right, but in that, they're fatally wrong. And where they're fundamentally wrong is in their assumption that they can simply slap a text onto a contemporary situation without understanding the deeper narrative and the deeper meaning of what's being dealt with in the text.

And so I want to go back and ask what was the world Jesus was in, what were the issues Jesus was facing, and how does his message make sense against that backdrop? And only after we've seriously engaged these questions can we begin to address the question of what that means for our context. So for me there are several intermediate steps between asking what are the crises and what does Jesus have to say to them. We've got to make sure we take those steps. Now obviously, in a two hundred page book, I can't do that in a very thorough way, but I hope I can at least introduce people into a way of imagining that being done.

TOJ: In the book you give a lot of attention to the relationship between Jesus's *kingdom of God* movement and the other movements of his day. How is this particular work an example of such an intermediary step, illuminating the way in which the Jesus of the Gospels can speak to contemporary crises?

BM: This is where it really gets interesting because I think it would be a serious mistake to assume that today's world is identical to Jesus's world. Yet I think what happens when you reflect upon these things, at least what happens for me, is that you really do begin to see similar themes. So you see the global economy or the American empire as having a lot in common with the Roman Empire in Jesus's day. And you see somebody like Osama bin Laden and his movement of al-Qaeda as having a lot in common with the Zealots. And you see a lot of our religious leaders having a lot in common with either the Sadducees or the Herodians, who in a sense side with Caesar, where the Pharisees end up siding with the Zealots. And then you see Jesus come onto the scene, and he has things in common with each of them, and he also diverges from each of them, so that in the end, all of them reject him. When he goes to the cross he is utterly alone as a failed would-be Messiah, and it looks like his movement is completely discredited. But here we are two thousand years later, and we believe that he was actually right and that God vindicated him through the resurrection. It's remarkable!

TOJ: In your book you distinguish between conventional and emerging views of the content of Jesus's kingdom message, the meaning of his death, and the nature of his return; the conventional view being dualistic—focusing on spiritual experiences and postmortem salvation—and the emerging view being holistic—emphasizing the unity of personal, social, and global transformation in both this life and the life to come. Now, if (as you indicate) some of our best theologians have been teaching the emerging view for quite some time, why is the evangelical consensus still characterized by the conventional view? Why is there such a gap between the evangelical theologian and the average evangelical? And if not the theologians, who's responsible for the shape of evangelicalism?

BM: To me this is where life gets really interesting because there are many layers to this and many things going on. Part of what we are dealing with is the reality of media, of mass media. So who has the most influence on the average teenager in America today, our most brilliant scholars or Britney Spears? And what Britney Spears—and you know, add any other name here—is to popular culture, some (not all!) radio preachers and televangelists can be to religious subculture.

Now I'm not making a one-to-one connection here. But what I am saying is that the people who control the popular media end up having massive influence, and they're quite disconnected from the scholars. In fact, you might even say that while scholars often are searching for what's true and real, popular media are simply responding to what's popular, and frankly, in religious broadcasting, what people will make donations to sustain.

So there's kind of a democratization of popular religious media that creates what I call an echo chamber. People want to hear about a subject, so the preachers talk about it because when they talk about it, people send them donations, so they talk all the more about it. So, for example, what we need to do to help the poor is not a really popular subject in religious broadcasting these days. Now, maybe because of my book and other people's work, people might begin to call in and say, "Hey, we want you to talk about how to help the poor," and then that can change.

So I'm not against religious media at all, and you know, wouldn't life be easy if we could just say, "This is good, and this is bad." But again, a lot of my background is Reformed, and total depravity tells me that I should expect corruption to sneak into every sector of life, including my own life. So take a doctrine like the dictation theory of inspiration, and here's where life gets interesting, because now we are in this cultural struggle with Islam, and Islam does hold to a dictation theory of the Koran. So here's the question: will our engagement with Islam make us revert to a dictation theory of inspiration in order to counter the Muslim message, or will it force us to become more sophisticated and mature in our understanding of the scriptures?

69

TOJ: It seems that a similar example is when the Catholic Church *reverted* to the doctrine of papal infallibility in response to the Protestant doctrine of the infallibility of the scriptures. Rather than both traditions taking it as an opportunity to develop, as you say, a more sophisticated and mature understanding of authority, they simply radicalized in order to outdo each other.

BM: Beautiful example. And of course, this is one of the other struggles currently under way—how do we talk about authority? Some of my fundamentalist colleagues say that the only way to have authority is to have certainty. Well, in their system that may be the only way to have authority, but we've seen the downside of certainty that is incapable of taking critique.

Now, once again, all of this is very, very dynamic, and this is one of the reasons we all have to be charitable with each other, because we're all in the midst of this; we are all trying to make do in a situation of huge change. And we don't all know the stories of where the ideas that we hold come from. We don't seem to understand that we are at point seventeen in a discussion that was going on long before we came on the scene and will be going on long after we're gone. Rather, we think it's all starting with us.

TOJ: Your book isn't only inviting evangelicals to get involved in God's world but also to get involved in a certain sort of way. For example, the Religious Right is already engaged, but their agenda and methods are far from what you commend to your readers. You also argue that "eschatology always wins," meaning that what one sees as the crises of our times and how one believes we ought to address them will be determined by whether one subscribes to the conventional or emerging eschatology. I am wondering what you might have to say to the evangelical who subscribes to the conventional view, but who really does want to be meaningfully engaged in God's world? Will the conventional view necessarily manifest itself in neoconservative politics?

BM: Well, there really is a link between neoconservative politics and the conventional view of eschatology. And of course, our conventional view is completely novel—nobody held a premillennial dispensationalist view before the 1830s. The emergent view is returning to the Church's historical view. What I would say is that I am worried that a misunderstanding of the second coming of Jesus is edging out the priority of the first coming of Jesus. And I want to make sure we give sufficient due to the first coming of Jesus.

So I believe in the ancient creeds, but isn't it interesting that our creeds say: "I believe in Jesus Christ . . . born of the Virgin Mary, suffered under Pontius Pilate . . . " and they skip over everything in-between? Well, that stuff in between was really important to Matthew, Mark, Luke, and John. Of course, Jesus's death and resurrection were very important to the four of them too, but so was his life. And in many ways, I think this is one of the deepest things going on. I think we've gotten offtrack. And I know a lot of people call me a heretic or whatever, but I actually think we've gotten off track, and I'm trying to get us back on track. And the way we've gotten off track is by the voice of Jesus being marginalized in our churches, largely because of a problematic eschatology, and I want us to hear the voice of Jesus and to allow what we hear to shape the way we live and love in God's world.

TOJ: The idea of a common good gets strong play in your book. You argue that a truly biblical Christianity will be concerned with the this-worldly social, economic, and political well-being of all God's creatures (regardless of their particular religious identity). In our religiously polarized time, is the very notion of the common good in crisis?

BM: I'm glad you picked up on this. One of the ways I think our Western Christian traditions have gotten into trouble is through a syncretism of the Gospel and colonialism—the Gospel and white (or Eurocentric) supremacy. This line of thinking creates an us-versus-them mind-set—us versus the other. But I think a more truly biblical view is an us-for-them mind-set, an us-for-the-other that sees not cleanliness but otherliness as next to godliness.

So Jesus tells us to love God and to love our neighbor, and then he extends the definition of neighbor to mean the other—the Samaritan, the whore, the drunk, even the Roman centurion and the enemy. It's one of the most radical dimensions of the Gospel. It's a major part of the scandal of the Gospel, but we pretty effectively neutralize that scandal, tragically.

TOJ: Returning to the notion that eschatology wins, I am curious to hear your thoughts on how certain eschatological views might work for or against Christian concern for the common good, as well as what other theological resources you'd highlight to help us realize that we really are all in the same boat as human beings before God?

BM: This is a huge question, and I imagine I'll be grappling with this for years to come, because I think I'm only scratching the surface. I deal with this a bit in my book *The Last Word and the Word After That* and in *Everything Must Change*, and it keeps coming back. Let me just give one example. This week, news came out that while our government was telling us they don't use torture, they were—secretly—using torture. Now if you believe, as Psalm 145:8–9 says, that God is ultimately compassionate, it becomes very hard to justify torture. But if you believe that the story of God ends with a large portion of God's creation experiencing eternal, conscious torture of unimaginable proportions, then somehow torture can't be that bad, because God does it, and never plans to stop. My friends who are deeply and irrevocably committed to the doctrine of eternal conscious torment need, I think, to realize this danger and to take preemptive action so that this doctrine won't be used by governments to do unconscionable acts. Or I should say, so that these acts, which are now in fact being done, will be stopped.

TOJ: In a time when arguments are flying back and forth like bombs that religion is either an unequivocal good or an unnecessary evil, your work has been refreshing to many, particularly to those of us (Christians and non-Christians alike) who don't identify with a traditional understanding of what it means to be religious. In your book, you draw attention to the fact that religion can function either for good or for ill, and you suggest that religion, including the Christian religion, is better understood in the very broad sense as a way of life rather than something immediately associated with an institution (church) or set of beliefs (theology). Could it be that by thinking of religion in terms of beliefs (about God) rather than as a way (of life), many Christians are operating with an unbiblical view of religion?

BM: Of course. These two can't be separated, nor should they be. But I think we have a problem in our status quo, where, to use Dallas Willard's image, a lot of people have a bar-code approach to faith. At death, God will scan our brains to see if we have the bar code of certain beliefs, and if we do, we go into the grocery bag of heaven. If not, we go into the trash bag of hell. That is a travesty of Jesus's actual teaching. Jesus called people to follow him, and he said he was the way, truth, and life. So as I see it, we are called to follow a way of life, and that way of life is and must be a way of fidelity to truth.

I sometimes find it helpful to replace the word *truth* with the word *reality*. Jesus says, "I am the way, the reality, the life," and we need to follow him, being faithful to the way he leads, the reality he manifests, and the life he shares.

TOJ: What criteria, biblical or otherwise, are available for discerning whether a given religion is indeed functioning for good or for ill?

BM: I don't think I have an easy litmus test, but your question brings to mind Jesus's words about good trees and good fruit, bad trees and bad fruit. So we might let the prophet Micah help us: is this religion drawing people to do justice, love kindness, and walk humbly with God? Or we might let Jesus define it as love for God and love for neighbor, stranger, and enemy. Or we might let Paul boil it down, as he does in Galatians, to "the only thing that counts is faith working through love."

Now I'm not saying that every religion that results in these fruits is equally good or true. But if we're looking for fruit, these kinds of things should be good signs. And if we see their opposite—I think of Paul's words, again from Galatians—we should be suspicious. Things like sexual immorality and debauchery, idolatry, hatred, discord, jealousy, ambition, dissensions, factions, envy, drunkenness, orgies, and so on.

Of course, as a follower of Jesus, for me being centered on Jesus is absolutely central, but because of what Jesus himself teaches, I can't be satisfied with a religion that sings and preaches Jesus but bears bad fruit. Nor can I be satisfied with a religion that bears good fruit but ignores Jesus.

TOJ: And how is the Christian religion faring on this front? You hint that Christianity is a failed religion. In what way has Christianity failed?

BM: Well, I think what I say is that many people see Christianity as a failed religion, and we Christians must face the evidence they can point to. We shouldn't be defensive; we should be humbled. Of course, the Gospels set us up for this—the disciples are constantly clueless. They're sending children away, telling people to shut up and go home, getting ready to call fire down from heaven on other people. The Gospels never lead us to believe that the disciples are going to be all that stellar. It's God in Christ who is reconciling the world, not us.

TOJ: Many people seem to doubt that it's possible to be both deeply committed to and deeply critical of one's religion. Yet you seem to argue that commitment and critique should go hand in hand and that there is room within Christianity for something like a critique of Christianity for Christ's sake.

BM: I like the way you say this. Our loyalty to Christ requires us to be critical of this or that expression of Christianity where it betrays Christ. Jesus, of course, does this in relation to his own religion—Judaism—as do all the prophets. It's their loyalty to God that makes them speak out against priests who give sacrifices according to the law but forget the widow and orphan.

TOJ: Turning from one controversial term to another, I'm eager to see what impact your book will have on the debate over evangelical identity (and the proper *marks* of an evangelical) that has been going on for the past few years. My sense is that those of us who are dissatisfied with the current definitions could rally around the notion of *evangelion* (or good news) that you explore in your book. In this way, being an evangelical would mean something like believing in the good news that God overcame the dis-ease within our world through Jesus of Nazareth, and that humanity can now take up its role again as those called to fill the world with justice and love.

I admit this is a far cry from those who want to establish evangelical identity according to a particular religious experience, usually a common conversion experience, or a particular doctrine of scripture, end times, or the atonement, but I am curious to hear your thoughts on how your book might contribute to the development of a more generous and worldly understanding of what it means to be an evangelical?

BM: My honest feeling is that this is a great question, but I'm not the best person to ask this of. I would think that people who are more invested in the term "evangelical" should be having this conversation. I think people who love the term "Reformed" also need to have this conversation, because very different understandings of faith coexist within that term, some of which I think are glorious and others less so.

My real calling, as I understand it, is not to be primarily an evangelical reformer. At heart, I'm an evangelist, and I'm hoping to call as many people to be followers of Jesus as I can, whatever tent they go into at night, whether it's the evangelical tent, the Mainline or Catholic or Orthodox tent, or some little lean-to with no name on it at all.

TOJ: If anything, evangelicals consider themselves Gospel-people, yet you've invited your readers to reconsider the very meaning of the Gospel— as an announcement of the renewal of God's creation rather than a technique for how one gets saved. This alone requires a deep shift in foundational evangelical assumptions about the message of Jesus.

BM: Yes, but I don't think a lot of people will see it that way. So many people seem completely incapable of even considering the remotest possibility that their understanding of the Gospel isn't already one hundred percent correct.

TOJ: In what way could such a notion of the evangelion be the basis for a new ecumenicism, where it might be no more surprising to hear someone refer to themselves as an evangelical Catholic or evangelical Orthodox than as an evangelical Protestant?

BM: You've articulated exactly my preferred understanding. I think the Gospel should be our guiding star, and we should live that out wherever we are called, whether that's in an evangelical, Catholic, Orthodox or whatever community. My hope is that we'll see a growing convergence of evangelical evangelicals, evangelical traditional Protestants, evangelical Catholics, and others—evangelical in this integral, holistic sense.

TOJ: You describe the journey you've been on for the last ten years or so as discovering and conversing about what it means to be a new kind of Christian, which is something other than a reactionary fundamentalist, a stuffy traditionalist, a blasé nominalist, a wishy-washy liberal, a New-Agey religious hipster, a crusading religious imperialist, or an overly enthused Bible-waving fanatic. You are candid about the fact that this book is written primarily for those already dissatisfied with conventional Christianity in any of its aforementioned forms, yet we can safely assume that many conventional types will read your book as well. What do you hope their response will be?

BM: Here would be my dream: that, for example, some of my highly conservative Reformed critics or some of my loyal *Left Behind* critics or prosperity-gospel critics would say, "You know, we think McLaren is pretty much an idiot and a fool. But he does raise some important questions. What are we going to do for the planet? What are we going to do for the poor? What are we going to do for peace-making? Because even though we think Brian is stupid and wrong, Jesus does care about these things, and because we love Jesus, we need to care too." That would be wonderful.

The way I say it in the book is something like this: some of us are questioning the theological contract we've been given—the belief system we've inherited. But others will not—and probably should not—question their theological contract. What they'll do is add fine print to it to make it more compassionate, humane, and responsible. If that happens, I'm overjoyed. I have pretty low expectations, I suppose. Or maybe those are still unreasonably high.

TOJ: Moving from dreams to reality [*smile*], do you think your book will be received by these folks who are resistant to a new kind of Christianity?

BM: Most people will ignore it, I imagine. They'll be told by their leaders that it is wrong and dangerous, so they'll steer clear, which is probably good because it's probably not the right book at the right time for them anyway. Some have already started to go after it. What saddens me is that they seem to skip over all the issues I raise about poverty, about planetary plundering, about an addiction to war, and they focus on a few things they disagree with. I can't believe that they can just skip over these other issues, but that's what some of them seem to do. It feels like straining gnats and swallowing camels to me, but I guess this is what will happen. I'm more hopeful for the children and grandchildren of these folks; maybe my books will help them after I'm buried under a tree somewhere.

TOJ: It's well known that fear is one of the biggest motivators, and well, let's just say many of your critics seem to be highly motivated. How would you rate the fear factor in all this, particularly among those who see themselves as the guardians of conventional Christianity?

BM: Some people are trusted by their communities to be watchdogs. They fulfill this role by taking their communities' established standards and testing everyone who comes along by these established standards. So *Left Behind* guardians will say, "He doesn't believe in our form of dispensationalism. He's bad. Avoid him." Prosperity-gospel folks will say something similar, and so on. This is certainly a legitimate task. Some are more fair than others. But none of them are able to say, "This book has me questioning some of our established standards," because the second they do so, they will be under attack by their fellow watchdogs, and there is so much fear in so many of our religious settings. It creates a kind of pathology, where people think, "I'm either going to be a suspect or an interrogator. I'll either be an inquisitor or I'll be held for questioning." It's very intimidating, even oppressive, at least to me. I guess some people like it; otherwise they'd leave.

TOJ: Speaking of watchdogs and interrogations, it seems that one of the challenges associated with making the case for the legitimacy of what is coming to be called progressive evangelicalism is that your more out-spoken critics repeatedly attempt to locate and confine you within one of the styles of Christianity you are attempting to differentiate from—unsur-prisingly, usually the one they are already most critical of for one reason or another. Perhaps this simply goes with the territory of attempting to articulate something new or that is currently emerging—it is simply in-terpreted within familiar, existing categories. So reactionary fundamental-ists refer to you as a New Agey religious hipster or a wishy-washy liberal, whereas wishy-washy liberals refer to you as a stuffy traditionalist or an enthused Bible-waving fanatic.

BM: Yes, you've just described my life in the blogosphere. There are a mil-lion legitimate criticisms to make of my work. We're all open to criticism. But what saddens me is that people are so quick to turn one another into enemies. My feeling is that we can all learn something from one another if we approach one another speaking truth in love.

TOJ: Okay bloggers, listen to this once and for all [*smile*]: how would you differentiate progressive evangelicalism from both liberalism and funda-mentalism? And how does it posture itself with respect to the long-stand-ing divide between these two main trajectories within North American Protestantism?

BM: You ask good questions, but my guess is that it would take a long book to do that question justice. Here's what I think is happening. I didn't start this; I'm just a small part of something that's been brewing for a long time. I mean, really, people like me are just picking up insights and themes from Luther, even Calvin, from Kierkegaard, from Walter Rauschenbusch, from Dr. King and Desmond Tutu, from Nancey Murphy and René Padilla and N. T. Wright and Jim Wallis and Tony Campolo and Diana Butler Bass, and so many others. These things have been brewing for a while and a kind of convergence is happening, drawing together those you're calling progressive evangelicals, those I would call postliberal mainliners, and progressive Catholics and Orthodox too.

This convergence is a kind of common ground, so we're less interested in distinguishing ourselves from others than we are in emphasizing our commonality with them and inviting them into conversation. I have no interest in being part of some sect, creating a new us-versus-them. Some people's reactions make that more likely; they label and exclude and vilify and so on, which can make people in my situation defensive so that we create our own little us-versus-them circle. But you see, my understanding of the Gospel of Jesus Christ makes me see that kind of us-versus-them thinking as part of the problem.

I believe that when Jesus died on the cross, he didn't say, "God, now you see who the bad guys are. Let them have it," but he said, "Father, forgive them. They don't know what they're doing." He was us-for-them even on the cross, and that's what I hope more and more of us can be. It's not easy. Jesus was labeled a friend of drunks and sinners. What could he do? He couldn't say, "No, I'm not! I hate drunks and sinners!" He had to let that label be used, and he just went on with his business, trusting God to sort it all out.

So if I'm labeled a friend of liberals, that's true; I am. And I'm also a friend of conservatives. I have a lot of great things to say about the prosperity-gospel and the *Left Behind* eschatology too, even though I'm critical of some dimensions of each. At the end of the day, we're all in this together. We're all trying to do what's right. And we all need a boatload of grace and mercy because we're all a mess, even at our best moments. At least that's how I see it.

TOJ: One of the things I appreciate most about your book is that you aren't simply addressing local churches, but you are calling individuals, families, neighborhood associations, community organizations, businesses, and governmental bodies all to address our world's crises in the unique ways that each of them are able. That said, a good way to draw our interview to a close would be to hear your thoughts on what it might look like if one or two of these groups took your book to heart.

BM: That's a fantastic way to end the interview, because this is what I really hope will happen. I don't offer a simple, "Here are three steps to take," at the end of the book. Instead, I offer one step, which is very deep and very hard and also very simple and very powerful. When people take that step, I hope they'll go to my website, www.brianmclaren.net, where we'll be putting together an auxiliary blog that invites people to share ideas on what to do to put the book into action. I think this is exciting because there are so many small ways we can respond, and together these small ways can create something quite transformative if they flow from faith.

Mountains can be moved with faith.

TOJ: We like to give our conversation partners space for any final comments. Any parting thoughts?

BM: Just thanks for asking such thoughtful questions. In a world of sound bites, it's really refreshing to have some substantive dialogue. Thanks for really engaging with the book. As you know, it's so important to me that people will take seriously the two questions we started with—what's going on in our world, and what does Jesus's message have to say about it? Because the problems are real and critical, and Jesus's words are good and true.

chapter 9

Uprising

by Becky Crook

The shirtless and barefoot people of
the earth are rising up as never before.
—MARTIN LUTHER KING JR.

The shirtless and barefoot people of the earth
are rising up as never before
and they walk past signs that say NO SERVICE
and they walk past lines of DON'T GO BEYOND.
They are rising up, they are rising up,
unashamed to wear their skin in the light,
an aberration to the thickly-robed,
and, as though in flight, their shoeless soles
gently kiss the famished ground,
stir up unnerving absence of
familiar scrape and shuffling sounds—
the click on pavement of captive feet.
And with chests of hair or breasts heaving—
appalling reminder of muscle beneath
(sinews contracting, valves opening doors)
—they're moving, they're stretching across the earth.
As never before, as never before,
the once-familiar geography's shifting:
straight yellow lines curl into spirals,
cold jagged glaciers carve trails through the plains,
craggy terrain forms a still, windless water.

And they walk through the land in the other direction,
scattering boulders as though they were seeds,
turning out graves and composting kings,
pausing to watch the freckled wings of
sparrows as they feed their young.
It's only beginning, it's only beginning.
They sing from the silence a beautiful song
about little things and small, unknown places,
the surprise that tomorrow came one day ahead.
We hear them sing as they go on their way,
and we are afraid.
We are afraid.

chapter 10

Britney Spears and the Downward Arc of Empire

An Interview with Eugene McCarraher

by Chris Keller

The Other Journal (*TOJ*): Let's start with Britney Spears, who was in the news all last week with *experts* decrying her parenting gaffes and bemoaning the fact that she has fallen so far that a judge would shift parental control from her to her burnout ex-husband K-Fed. Putting aside questions of why this is news and what is news, how do you account for our culture's nurturing of celebrity that seems to fluctuate between consuming (Britney as sex symbol) and discarding (Britney as burnout mom), between lust and contempt? Are we are seeing celebrities as commodities, and if so, what does this phenomena say about us and how we relate to one another as consumers?

Eugene McCarraher (EM): I don't think you can put aside the question of why Britney Spears is news because ignoring it means we're ignoring the production end of celebrity. Like the rest of the news, Ms. Spears is a product of the culture industry, one of whose chief purposes is to distract us from the tedium or injustice of our daily lives. Just as her pre-meltdown songs and videos were glittery commodified ephemera, created precisely for the purpose of being enjoyed and discarded, so her meltdown is a commodity, mediated for our entertainment pleasure.

But on top of that, Ms. Spears is a commodity fetish, to use Marx's still-relevant and illuminating language. Like any other commodity fetish, Ms. Spears is a screen onto whom consumers project their own repressed desires—in her case, to misbehave. And like many a repressed desire, its inexorable expression is malignant. Seeing its malignancy, consumers deride their fetish, often with

83

a viciousness commensurate to the intensity of the identification with the commodity. So there's something insidious, not only about the consumption of her sexualized persona, but about the way that celebrities-in-distress like Ms. Spears are tossed aside. The celebrity cycle of consumption-disappointment-vicious rejection raises to a high degree of visibility and vividness the way in which all goods are handled in this culture. Unable or unwilling to confront their desires for what they are, or to discover how to transform those desires in accordance with their status as, oh, the *imago Dei*, consumers project [their desires] onto commodities, suffer [. . .] inevitable lack of fulfillment, and grow ever more cynical and full of rage. The telos of consumer autonomy turns out to be not so much freedom or license as a sullen emptiness and boredom that eventually requires different forms of violence—verbal, visual, military—for its satisfaction.

TOJ: So given the importance of what is news, do you understand our national obsession with sports in a similar light, as a commodity meant to distract us from the deeper injustices that plague our lives, similar I suppose to imperial Rome (gladiators, coliseum, et cetera)?

EM: Yes, but sports also retain some potential as a source of criticism of commodity culture. On the one hand, sports sell both capitalism and nationalism: during a typical football broadcast, for instance, you'll get a standard ideological package of beer, food, cars, sexual titillation, and some patriotism thrown in. ("Are you ready for some U.S.A.?") But because even professionalized, commodified sports still insist both on achievement within rules and on standards of excellence that have nothing to do with money, they represent an oasis of sorts within the culture of avarice.

TOJ: You have argued that our culture in North America is one that thrives on death, "from poverty, unemployment, and alienation, to abortion, capitol punishment, and war," and that as Christians our most urgent duty is the affirmation of life. What do we, in the fall of 2007, urgently need to be doing to affirm life? Furthermore, if we are really to affirm life, how do we disinfect ourselves of the pervading *libido dominandi,* which you describe as "the love of domination, which corrupts everything we are and create"?

EM: On one level, it's quite simple: don't participate in wars; don't have an abortion; protest the state-sponsored murder of offenders; create an economy that provides useful, remunerative, and cooperative employment.

But clearly there's more involved. First, Christians should practice the fundamentals: the sacraments, prayer, study of scripture and tradition. As the defining practices of Christian faith, they're the template for a culture of life, as they afford both participation in the divine life and the growing realization of what a gift life is, not something we have to *earn* or *deserve*. So much of *libido dominandi* is traceable to our acting as though we have to gain God's approval or to acting as though we or others must be *wanted* or that we should *deserve* life—or death. (Father Herbert McCabe has some wonderful passages in his sermons on all of this.)

Some of the other advice I'd offer probably won't go down as easily. First, I think that Christians should stop yakking about consumerism. Consumerism is not the problem—capitalism is. Consumerism is the work ethic of consumption, the transformation of leisure and pleasure into duties. Talking about consumerism is a way of not talking about capitalism, and I've come to think that that's the reason why so many people, including Christians, whine about it so much. It's just too easy a target. There's a long history behind this, but the creation of consumer culture is very much about compensating workers for loss of control and creativity at work, and those things were stolen because capital needed to subject workers to industrial discipline. (I don't, by the way, believe that we inhabit a post-industrial society. Our current regimes of work are, indeed, super-industrial.) Telling people that they're materialistic is both tiresome and wrong-headed: tiresome because it clearly doesn't work, and wrong-headed because it gives people the impression that matter and spirit are antithetical. As Christians, we should be reminding everyone that material reality is sacramental, and that therefore material production, exchange, and consumption can be ways of mediating the divine.

As for abortion, I think we have to stop seeing it as the primary culprit in a *culture of death*. Abortion becomes conceivable as a moral practice once we take individual autonomy as the beau ideal of the self; but to recognize that is, if we're logical, to indict not only abortion but also our cherished idyll of choice or freedom. But that, then, is to indict capitalism, which employs a similar language of sovereignty both to legitimate itself and to obscure the remarkable lack of creative freedom at work. I know that I'll catch a lot of hell for saying this, but I think that a lot of opposition to abortion is sheer moral sentimentality which turns the fetus into a fetish. (You'll notice that I think fetishism of some sort or other is a pretty salient feature of the contemporary American moral imagination.) Many of the same people who oppose abortion are champions of laissez-faire capitalism, and they either don't see or don't care to see the linguistic and cultural affinities between themselves and the pro-choice advocates they fight. They'll retort that capitalism doesn't kill anyone in its normal operations, but first, that's just not true—capitalism has never been instituted or maintained anywhere, not even in the North Atlantic, without considerable coercion and violence—and second, it doesn't matter, because the exercise of market autonomy has devastating effects on individuals and communities regardless of whether or not they wind up dead. ("Yeah, the company cut your medical benefits or cut your job or left your town a mess, but hey, you're still alive!") When I say this, a lot of people retort that I'm changing the subject. In one way, yes, I am, but for a reason—because I want them to see that it is the same subject in a different guise. Talking about abortion is a way of not talking about the autonomous individual, the latest ideological guise of *libido dominandi*, discussion of which would topple quite a few idols and not just *reproductive choice*.

As for talk about empire, it can obscure the fact that, while the U.S. is indisputably an empire, it's also an empire in decline. If the American empire were as strong as the rhetoric of many Christians makes it out to be, there'd be no point in doing anything other than retreating into ecclesial enclaves, talking sagely about *practices*, and—oh, gee, that's what a lot of theologians and pastors and seminarians are doing. But if, as I believe, the empire is now on the downward slope of its historical arc, then Christians can be optimistic as well as hopeful. (Yes, there's a difference, but many then go on to think that optimism is always foolish. It isn't.) Although I don't believe that we'll be leaving Iraq any time soon—since we invaded for the oil and for geo-political advantage, it stands to reason that we're not going to exit—it's also quite apparent that the insurgency, together with the lack of genuine domestic support (how many war enthusiasts do you know who've enlisted out of patriotic fervor?), have demonstrated the limits of our vaunted military might. Moreover, the extremely fragile state of finance capital, the knowledge that we can't rely on oil for much longer to propel our corporate consumer economy—all of that should indicate that the empire is very much in the condition of Edwardian England, or Hapsburg Spain, or fourth- to fifth-century Rome.

Given that we're an empire on the downslope, Christians should be preaching the good news that America can decline gracefully, and that Americans will be saner and happier when they relinquish the imperial imperative. (I have no patience with the providentialist bullshit shoveled by Father Richard John Neuhaus or Stephen Webb. That star-spangled drivel has gotten and will continue to get a lot of people killed.) Talking about empire is a way of not talking about the world we could build in concert with the many non-Christians who also see the impending erosion of American power.

So what, then, should Christians do to create a culture of life? If economics is part of a culture of life, then we need a political economy of life. And I am unashamed in saying that some form of socialism remains the most inspiring and practical way of arranging our economic affairs in the light of the Gospel. We should wind our way back to the road not taken in the late-nineteenth and early-twentieth century: Christian socialism, which now has to be a post-secular socialism, undertaken in concert with non-Christians. Work to transform capitalism, not into a more efficient way of producing and distributing "illth," as John Ruskin called so much of the shabby and dangerous and unedifying "crapola" that truly is a gross domestic product, but into a political economy of genuine wealth, "the possession of the valuable by the valiant." At a minimum, that means a metamorphosis in the ethos and curricula of business and professional schools at Christian colleges and universities. Christians should be pioneering a whole new economics, not just tacking values onto capitalism. They should be affirming abundance, not scarcity, as the primary ontological fact of economics. They should be offering courses not in management but in how to do without management as a distinct class. They should be offering courses and training in union organization, or in dispossessing those useless people otherwise known as stockholders and putting firms into the hands of people who actually work in them.

I'm convinced that working toward such a political economy of life would increasingly render abortion more and more inconceivable for the simple reason that *libido dominandi* wouldn't leaven the entire society.

TOJ: In this issue, we are looking at psychopathology and sin—what sins define our culture? How are they deforming our psyches and our hearts? Are they representative of acute psychopathologies or broader personality deformations? One of the foundational questions then, in approaching this topic, and one that indeed undergirds psychology and politics, is how do we conceive of the self? Within our modern political discourse, how do our views of freedom and inalienable rights fashion the idea of the secular self? How is the late-capitalist, secular self at odds with the Christian account of personhood?

EM: I don't believe that the modern self is secular, at least not in the way that's usually understood, and I don't believe it because, however deeply deformed we become, we're still the *imago Dei*, and that means that we're always yearning, even despite ourselves, to participate in the divine life. In discussions of the person as well as in discussions of history, economics, et cetera, it's absolutely crucial to not give an inch to the secularization narrative, because to the extent that you do, you surrender any serious claim on the disputed territory. Once you concede the essential legitimacy of the secular account of the person—or of economics, or politics, et cetera—you end up relegating Christianity to the realm of spirituality or values or some other gaseous invertebrate that hovers around an essentially secular self. Rather, Christians should contend that the secular marks the repression, displacement, and renaming of our desire for a sacramental way of being in the world. Indeed, the history of the person is both the history of those perversions and of attempts to mitigate or undo the perversions. So I think that it's better to say not that the Christian account of personhood is at odds with the secular account, [but that] the secular account is a disfigurement of personhood.

In this view, the self under late capitalism is a perversion of our desires for a beloved, sacramental community of labor. If you look closely, I think you'll find that, for instance, a great deal of management theory—as dullard or cynical as it truly is—represents an effort on the part of corporate capital to simulate such a community. Advertising, to take another example, is the devotional iconography of late capitalism: it arouses, in the very act of disfiguring, our sacramental longing for a land of milk and honey, for a New Jerusalem.

All that said, I've come to dissent somewhat from William Cavanaugh and Stanley Hauerwas and John Milbank and others who see almost nothing but perniciousness in the liberal tradition. Look, let's be honest: the heroes of the antislavery movement, of the movements for women's rights and for civil rights for nonwhites, all employed the language of liberalism in addition to the language of Christianity. Why? In large measure, because Christian tradition had legitimated a language of hierarchy and duty and subordination that even Cavanaugh and Hauerwas and Milbank can't stomach anymore. Perhaps because I'm a mere historian, I have to respect the indisputable evidence that Christians certainly weren't citing the church fathers when they demanded that the slaves' shackles be loosened or that women get the right to vote and be educated. For all that, it's perverted the Christian account of personhood, the liberal account of freedom and rights has preserved and, yes, even enhanced vestiges of the Christian tradition. So enough liberal-bashing; it has gotten boring, and it's not entirely accurate historically, anyway.

TOJ: The Gates Foundation, powered with staggering capital from Bill Gates's fortune as well Warren Buffett's billions, promises to do what governments in the developing world have not been able to do, things such as eradicate malaria in the third world and provide aid to the poorest of the poor. Two of the richest men in the world, who have thrived in the marketplace and become inconceivably wealthy from corporate profit, seem to be following the soteriological script of capitalism to a tee—a script that says eventually wealth will trickle down, aid the needy, and the market will mete out justice. (Such crises in Africa and generally in the developing world are terrible situations, and I am, like everyone else, relieved to see mosquito nets distributed and vaccines being tested to eradicate malaria, a disease that kills one million impoverished people a year.) How can we understand the Gates Foundation phenomena in light of your statement that "a vital task of any genuinely pro-life gospel and politics should be the demolition of the corporation's material and cultural power"?

EM: I think we must understand the Gates Foundation in exactly the way you described it: as a capitalist soteriology. That's a basically Augustinian way to frame it, and as Augustine says, not everything about the earthly city is rotten. Still, even compassionate actions are performed with the ultimate intention of preserving and extending the *libido dominandi* that propels the earthly realm, and those actions are inevitably further compromised by the conditions that made them necessary and possible. There is, for instance, a correlation between Western economic policies and health pandemics. Witness, for instance, the infamous Bhopal incident in India a while back, caused by Union Carbide's reckless conduct. That wasn't just a correlation, but a direct cause-effect relationship. Moreover, there is clearly more than a correlation between the (often coerced) adoption of agri-capitalist practices (single-crop farming, the use of various pesticides and other chemicals, etc.) and large-scale famine.

What should also trouble us about the Gates-Buffett initiatives is the idea that the poor—or the rest of us, for that matter—should have to depend on the benefactions of the super-rich rather than on the ministrations of government or of religious institutions. These acts of *bourgeois-oblige*, so to speak, exemplify the utter privatization of public services, among which should be the provision of medical care. Indeed, Gates and Buffett are idols of the corporate-benevolence complex: these are people who exploit workers and extract resources and then shower benefits on the world's wretched, soaking up praise for their charitable endeavors. Thank you, thank you, oh nabobs of wealth, for deigning to notice our plight. So while Gates and Buffett's actions are certainly better than nothing, they shouldn't warm our hearts for too long.

TOJ: It is said that we live in a therapeutic culture and that psychotherapy has begun to supplement authentic community, intimate friendship, and authentic confession in the context of the church. Celebrities often erase past mistakes in a public-relations sense by going into rehab; therapeutic terms such as repression and projection are common within the parlance of our time; and the therapist's office has become somewhat of a holy place where authenticity and healing can thrive. As a Christian psychotherapist, I recognize the value of psychiatry and psychology. I also am often struck in a broader sense by the enabling nature of the psychiatric and psychological industries, where normalcy is subtly and not-so-subtly couched in terms of being free from suffering, and *being yourself* is prized regardless of vice or virtue. Are we a therapeutic culture? Is the account of wellness that the psychiatric and psychological industries are importing congruent with the therapeutics of the Gospel?

EM: The phrasing of your last question underscores why we have to be careful when using terms like "therapy" or "therapeutic culture." A lot of scholars often invoke Philip Rieff when trashing our therapeutic obsessions, but Rieff was much more meticulous and insightful in his use of these terms than a lot of his subsequent enthusiasts have been. Rieff is very clear, in *The Triumph of the Therapeutic*, that all cultures are therapeutic— that is, all have ways of forming personal identity and integrating it into the larger community. Rieff distinguished not between therapeutic and non-therapeutic cultures but between rival therapeutic modes and communities, their ideals of health and methods of cure. He also made a crucial distinction between positive therapeutic communities—which link interior well-being to commitments outside the self and seek a transformation of desires in accordance with certain communal purposes—and negative communities—[...] which lack integrating symbols and communal purposes and thus register rather than transform desires. In his view, the contemporary West was a negative or purely therapeutic community. (Rieff's prose can be maddeningly abstruse, and I think this is why it's easy to misread him.)

Now, I think Rieff's characterization of our culture as purely therapeutic is right as far as he goes, but I think we have to understand that Western capitalist democracies do, in fact, have an integrating purpose: the production and consumption of commodities. Rieff didn't clearly relate the triumph of the therapeutic to the cultural and psychic impact of capitalism—mainly, I suspect, because he comes out of a tradition of conservative cultural criticism which just doesn't like to dwell on capitalism. (They think it's reductive or Marxist or materialist—in short, it's bad intellectual manners—to mention economics.) Alasdair MacIntyre's association of the therapist and the manager in *After Virtue* highlights this connection.

In my view—and I used this to frame a good part of the argument in *Christian Critics*—*The Triumph of the Therapeutic* traces, not a shift from religion to therapy, but a transferal of therapeutic powers from religious authorities to secular experts, as well as an uncoupling of personal therapy from aspiration toward a broader collective destiny. That's not to say that Christians can't rely on psychological or psychiatric professionals—I certainly don't think that preaching the Gospel to people is a cure for obsessive-compulsive disorders or for schizophrenia or for any number of personal troubles. But I do think it's pretty obvious that many people, including Christians, now take certain troubles to mental health professionals that require more than talking cures or prescriptions. And I think they do so because the notion of cure that's at work is one very much like industrial efficiency: you do this, you take that, and you'll be free of whatever malady is bothering you. The Gospel doesn't assure you that you'll be cured of a certain malady; it proclaims that you're forgiven, not that you're free of any number of obsessions or sins.

TOJ: As you know, post–9/11, pro-atheism publications are plentiful and have often launched acerbic attacks on the Christian tradition. Is this a new intellectual current that you are seeing in the academy, which has primarily been nurtured by the Bush administration's religious language and the 9/11 attack by religious fundamentalists? Beyond the War on Terror and anti-Bush sentiments, why in 2007 are such publications wildly popular with the culture at large?

EM: Looking at these books in purely intellectual terms, I don't think that the current spate of anti-religious books indicates anything strikingly new. The arguments you get from Sam Harris or Richard Dawkins or Christopher Hitchens are basically the same arguments we heard from Voltaire, Marx, Nietzsche, [Charles] Bradlaugh, Ingersoll, [Madalyn Murray] O'Hair, et cetera: religion is scientifically absurd; it is sponsored superstition and slaughter, et cetera. What's new is the extent to which these arguments are now common currency among wide swaths of the upper-middle classes, who are, given the price of books these days, the primary audience for these writers. So I don't think this is simply an anti-Bush phenomenon, and I don't think it's simply a reaction to the religious right or to radical Islam. These sentiments have been out there for quite a while, and the vitality of fundamentalist religion has elicited a suitably exuberant reaction.

I also doubt that this is only a recoil from Bush and evangelicals because support for the new atheism doesn't necessarily translate into opposition to the War on Terror. Everyone knows that Hitchens has been an especially virulent and bloodthirsty warmonger; it's rather less well-known that Harris is also a stalwart supporter of the use of U.S. military power against terrorists. (As you and many of your readers may know, I wrote a long review of Hitchens's *God is Not Great* for *Commonweal* in which I explored these issues at some length.)

TOJ: In your Winter 2004 *The New Pantagruel* article, "Christian Intellectuals, Embedded and Otherwise," you gave a call to arms for Christian intellectuals, in which you said, "What is to be done? First, we must demolish unrelentingly the illusions promulgated by [Michael] Novak, [Jean] Elshtain, [George] Weigel, Neuhaus, and other embedded Christian intellectuals. Whether ignorant or heedless of American hubris, they sanitize their accounts of the imperial order; pervert the critical intelligence of Christian faith; and bivouac in the discursive parameters drawn by the corporate regime. Stale and obscurantist, their rendering unto Official Sources merits rebuke and inattention. It's time for regime change among Christian intellectuals."

Could you elaborate on the need for regime change using some recent examples of Christians sanitizing their accounts of the imperial order, and have you been encouraged by indicators of such a regime change among Christian intellectuals in the last three years?

EM: From a legion of disgrace, the two best-known examples of Christian fealty to empire have been Elshtain and Neuhaus. Elshtain's work had been heading in this direction for over a decade. Disturbed by some trends on the left, and especially among feminists, she appointed herself something of a Lady Bracknell to preside over cultural and political discourse. In the course of becoming an ideological cop, she morphed into one of these virtue- and civility-meisters, wagging her finger at everyone to mind their intellectual and polemical manners. She started seeming a lot like William Bennett, adopting this schoolmarmish, moralizing tone. Then along came 9/11 and Iraq, and she went over to the dark side, pontificating on Just War and spouting all sorts of Augustinian tautologies. Along with Michael Novak, she got to be one of the media's go-to people for a quick exposition of why God wants us to go to war. You don't hear much from her now that everything's gone down the crapper.

Neuhaus was always a bellicose sort, even when he was on the left. Like most other intellectuals who opine so sagely about Just War, he's a chickhawk whose relationship to violence has always been of the most conceptual and literary sort. (In *The Theocons*, Damon Linker traces Father Richard's attraction to violence.) Add to that his supine deference to *competent authorities*—this, from a man old enough to remember Tonkin, My Lai, and Cambodia—and you have the classic authoritarian personality.

Against the embedded Christians, I've been immensely encouraged by the emergence of a motley and diverse group of Christians unwilling to enlist their talents in the service of Caesar. When I read and talk to people like Bill Cavanaugh, Mike Budde, Shane Claiborne, Kelly Johnson, Charles Marsh, Lauren Winner, Richard Hays, or Steve Long—all of whom are indebted to Hauerwas and John Howard Yoder—I know there's hope, enormous hope.

TOJ: Finally, we usually leave open space at the end of our interview if you have any final thoughts you would like to share. Final thoughts?

EM: No. I think I've probably said quite enough to inspire, provoke, or anger your readers. My work here is done. Serenity now.

chapter 11

The ONE Campaign and Product (RED)

Revolution without Cost

by Sean Jackson

IN THE FALL of 2006, a new movement swept across North America. Promoted by the likes of Oprah and Bono, Matt and George, and Angelina and Brad, the ONE Campaign has quickly become the social cause to support. And with awareness for global poverty and disease at perhaps an all-time high, more and more people (almost 2.5 million actually)[1] have joined the ONE Campaign. With their unique purchasing power as first-world consumers, Americans can now interact with and respond to global crises in the fourth world (like disease, famine, and a lack of clean water) by purchasing products associated with ONE through the PRODUCT (RED) campaign.

But I have a confession to make: I have yet to buy a PRODUCT (RED) Nano iPod, a PRODUCT (RED) Moto Razr phone, or even a PRODUCT (RED) t-shirt from Gap. I have, however, been puzzling over this technique, known as cause marketing, for enticing us consumers to "make poverty history" by doing what we do best, consume.

In essence, the (RED) campaign allows us to alleviate our first-world guilt by buying specially marked items that may prolong the life of an AIDS victim in the fourth world. It's brilliant, is it not? People's lives are saved *and* we don't have to stop buying the things we probably don't need. PRODUCT (RED) is the perfect solution to one of consumer culture's nastier problems: what to do with the world's poor and suffering while maintaining our own opulent lifestyles.

Here is my question: Shouldn't helping be costly? If by purchasing an item that we want, we can help someone in need, what happens when we are

1. As shown on the front page at www.one.org.

asked to help without the promise of some shiny new toy? Suddenly, helping looks like, well, helping, and all that hype about impacting the life of another person is about as exciting as living with a life-changing illness. Where is the cost? Where is the sacrifice when we gain something in addition to the good health of a man or woman, boy or girl? The (RED) campaign is telling us something about ourselves that should give us pause. In an effort to bolster the bottom line, the (RED) campaign is telling us that life is *not* enough of a reason to care, and they have built a successful business model on this idea.

On the surface, it is difficult to criticize an attempt to raise money for those in need. But then I remember Jesus and his words to his followers:

> Watch out! Don't do your good deeds publicly, to be admired by others, for you will lose the reward from your father in heaven. When you give to someone in need, don't do as the hypocrites do—blowing trumpets in the synagogues and streets to call attention to their acts of charity! I tell you the truth, they have received all the reward they will ever get. But when you give to someone in need, don't let your left hand know what your right hand is doing. Give your gifts in private, and your Father, who sees everything, will reward you. (Matt 6:1–4 NIV)

Christ's words suggest that perhaps another attraction of the (RED) campaign is that in this marketing-saturated culture our specially marked (RED) products "trumpet" our desire to be admired, to be regarded as savvy and relevant.

The ONE Campaign boldly states that we can "make poverty history," that we can eradicate poverty in our world. But there is another implication in those three words that stirs something within us. As a culture accustomed to fixing problems, ONE's motto subtly implies that there can be an end to the problem of the poor and thus an end to the need to fix the problem. As someone put it to me in a recent conversation, "Who wants to sign up for something that never ends?" In other words, we all want to be a part of something that makes a lasting difference; we just don't want it to last very long. Yet serving the poor is costly and usually requires both our time and our money.

In Deuteronomy 15:7–10, God tells his people that if they "give generously" to the poor they will be blessed, but He also warns that ". . . there will always be some in the land who are poor." And in the Gospels of

Matthew, Mark, and John, Jesus tells us that we will always have the poor with us and that we can help them whenever we wish.

Like PRODUCT (RED), the ONE Campaign offers real hope in the wrappings of a false promise. It is good to hope for and desire the end of poverty. But it is only in the second coming of Jesus that we will see the end of poverty, not by our own efforts, but because all things have been redeemed and made ready for a new life by Jesus. ONE's campaign is deceptive because it sells short the costly, lifelong work of caring and providing for the poor.

Just as the problems of pain in our world are neither black nor white, it is also true that our attempts to help are neither right nor wrong. And while it may be true that some or even most of us are really more interested in our shiny new toy or a brief moment of admiration, there are also consumers who honestly wish to help someone in need. It is precisely for this reason that we cannot become entangled in causes that first define the problem and then sell us the answer. We must think deeply about the cost of helping those in need so that when we are faced with the choice of how to serve, we don't first require a tip.

chapter 12

What Is Wrong
with Capitalism?

The Problem with the

Problem with Capitalism

by Daniel M. Bell Jr.

Why do you labor for
that which does not satisfy?
—Isaiah 55:2

THE NOTED CHRISTIAN theologian Michael Novak has observed that "we are all capitalist now,"[1] and as I write these words, an evangelical Christian is beginning his second term in what is arguably the single most influential economic post in the world.[2] This should give us pause as we consider the question, "What is the problem of capitalism?" For it is not at all clear that capitalism and Christianity are at odds to any significant degree. Indeed, although evangelical Christians readily admit that capitalism should not be confused with the Kingdom of God, evangelicals—the believers who see themselves as adherents of the classic Christian faith—are some of the most fervent advocates of capitalism and its advance, and even capitalism's Christian detractors are inevitably capitalists. (Where do they shop? Where were their shirts made?)

Given this apparent complementarity of capitalism and Christianity, perhaps the first problem confronted when confronting the problem of capitalism is the problem with the problem of capitalism. What is the problem

1. Novak, *The Catholic Ethic*, 101.

2. Although President Bush has been identified as an evangelical Christian by many of his supporters as well as detractors, this identification, too, is debatable. See, for example, McGarvey, "As God is His Witness."

of the problem of capitalism? Capitalism's Christian advocates are pretty clear what the problem is: It is the vested interest that the ethics establishment has in denigrating all things (North) American, which it does by offering simplistic judgments of complex economic realities.[3] The problem is that theologians are out-of-date and downright medieval when it comes to matters economic.[4] There is, no doubt, some truth to these sorts of claims. For example, how much of our animus toward capital is really a self-serving maneuver to make a virtue of necessity? Academics, clergy, and other professional religious types, after all, are not typically found in the higher altitudes of the wage scale. And how many of us have taken the time to actually engage the discipline of economics instead of simply dismissing it?[5] How many of us know, for example, the difference between absolute and comparative advantage or that scarcity is a claim not so much about natural resources as it is about the psychological or desiring constitution of the human being?

In addition to these commonplace difficulties with Christian critiques of capitalism, there is another set of difficulties that is rarely recognized. Specifically, Christian critiques of capitalism are hindered because the problem of capitalism is typically posed empirically instead of confessionally, and it is posed empirically in a flawed manner.

What Is Wrong with the Question, "What Is Wrong with Capitalism?"

Engage someone in a conversation about capitalism. Ask them if it is good or bad, if it comports with Christian convictions. Invariably, the conversation or argument will revolve around the issue of whether or not capitalism works. More specifically, the question will turn—in endless circles of undoubtedly escalating rhetoric—on whether it aids the poor in escaping their poverty or abets the forces that perpetrate and perpetuate that poverty. This is a straightforward empirical argument, even if empirical evidence is rarely if ever able to settle such disputes. This empirical turn makes sense; it makes sense because there is near universal agreement

---

3. Benne, *The Ethic of Democratic Capitalism*, 5, 7.

4. Novak, "Changing the Paradigms," 180.

5. One contemporary theologian who stands out for his engagement with the discipline is D. Stephen Long. See his *Divine Economy*.

among Christians that concern for the poor and alleviating poverty is a proper task of the economic order. For example, advocates of capitalism and critics of such movements as Latin American liberation theology, which couples a prominent concern for the poor with a sharp critique of capitalism, readily agree with liberationists that God is especially concerned for the welfare of the poor. As Amy Sherman, a Christian advocate of capitalism, notes, "For Christians, opting for the poor is not optional; it is a clear command of Christ."[6]

Yet the empirical turn is flawed to the extent that it revolves solely around the question of whether or not capitalism works. This is the case because it is rather obvious that capitalism works. Indeed, one of the reasons it is lauded is precisely because it works as well as it does. This is to say, no economic order to date has so obviously displayed such an enormous productive capacity as has capitalism. Hence, the empirical question put to capitalism cannot be "does it work?" The obvious answer is "yes." Rather the empirical question should be "what work does it do?" Rethinking the empirical question in these terms makes a significant difference in how Christians might evaluate capitalism theologically, although that difference may not be readily apparent.

For instance, the difference made by posing the question of capitalism in terms of the work it does may not be obvious when I argue that a problem with capitalism is not that it does not work, but rather that the work that it does is not the work we should be doing with regard to caring for our neighbors and seeing to it that material things are produced and allocated in accord with their proper, divinely-ordained, universal destination (see John Paul II, *Centesimus Annus*). The difference that this reframing of the empirical question makes, however, comes into sharper focus when I argue that even if I am wrong and capitalism's chaplains are right, even if capitalism is actually on the whole advancing the cause of the poor and alleviating unjust suffering, it would still be wrong and rightly resisted. Why?

Because capitalism is wrong, not only on account of its failure to aid the poor and needy, but also because of what it does succeed in doing, namely, deforming human desire. As Augustine noted long ago, humans are created to desire God and the things of God. Capitalism corrupts desire. Even if capitalism succeeds in reducing poverty, it is still wrong on account of its distortion of human desire and human relations.

6. Sherman, *Preferential Option*, 219.

As Alasdair MacIntyre has noted, "Although Christian indictments of capitalism have justly focused attention upon the wrongs done to the poor and the exploited, Christianity has to view any social and economic order that treats being or becoming rich as highly desirable as doing wrong to those who must not only accept its goals, but succeed in achieving them. . . . Capitalism is bad for those who succeed by its standards as well as for those who fail by them, something that many preachers and theologians have failed to recognize."[7] Capitalism is wrong not simply because it *fails* to succor the impoverished, but also because where it *succeeds*, it deforms and corrupts human desire into an insatiable drive for more. Capitalism makes a virtue of what an earlier era denounced as a vice, *pleonexia*, or greed—a restless, possessive, acquisitive drive that today is celebrated as the aggressive, creative, entrepreneurial energy that distinguishes *homo economicus*.[8] Diagnoses and critiques of this cancerous desire and its effects abound and need not be repeated here.

However, not everyone succeeds under capitalism; not everyone is a successful apprentice and so attains the coveted mantle of consumer or entrepreneur. Indeed, as liberationists have pointed out in recent years, increasingly significant numbers of people are not so much oppressed by capitalism as they are excluded.[9] In other words, while capitalist discipline celebrates consumption, not all of its subjects are rightly called consumers. To the contrary, many who are subject to its discipline do not so much struggle to consume and accumulate as to merely survive, which suggests the second way capitalism works to deform humanity.

Not only does capitalism deform the desire of those who prosper or at least survive under its tutelage, it also distorts human relations, even the relationships of those who are excluded from its fruits. This is to say, even if capitalism elevated the poor, it would still be wrong on account of the way it corrupts human relations, rendering them antagonistic, competitive. Capitalism has so constructed the market that humans interact agonistically, competitively. All of us, winners and losers, consumers and excluded, compete for resources, for market shares, for living wages, for jobs, for the

7. MacIntyre, *Marxism and Christianity*, xiv.

8. See Hirschman, *The Passions and the Interests*; and Myers, *The Soul of Modern Economic Man*. See also MacIntyre, *Whose Justice? Which Rationality?*, 111–12; and MacPherson, *The Political Theory of Possessive Individualism*.

9. See, for example, Hinkelammert, *Cultura de la Esperanza y Sociedad sin Exclusión*.

time for friendship and family, for inclusion in the market, and so forth.[10] Capitalism is wrong because even if it delivers the goods, it nevertheless works against the good, corrupting (and perpetuating the corruption of) human sociality in competitive and conflictual modalities. Capitalism is wrong, not simply on the grounds of what it fails to do but because of what it succeeds in doing: distorting human desire and relations.

What Is the Alternative?

The argument I have advanced thus far has not actually advanced very far. This is because while Christian advocates of capitalism might argue with the particulars, they would not dispute the broader point, namely, that capitalism is *not* synonymous with Christianity. In this regard, Christian opponents of capitalism would do well to take down their straw figures and quit jousting with windmills (unless they are content preaching only to the choir). Few, if any, Christian proponents of capitalism contend that there is a straightforward and unproblematic interface between the two. Novak is not atypical in this regard when he writes, "Capitalism itself is not even close to being the kingdom of God . . . . The presuppositions, ethos, moral habits, and way of life required for the smooth functioning of democratic and capitalist institutions are not a full expression of Christian or Jewish faith, and are indeed partially in conflict with the full transcendent demands of Christian and Jewish faith."[11]

Rather, the argument that Christian proponents of capitalism consistently make is essentially that given the alternatives, capitalism, warts and all, is the best that we can do. In other words, the rejoinder to capitalism's critics is simply and powerfully, what is the better alternative?

The answers have not proven particularly compelling. For a long time, Christian opponents of capitalism were bold in their assertions that socialism was the alternative, and for a while (in the midst of the global revolutionary climate that blossomed in the 1960s and lingered into the '80s) that conviction was at least understandable. In more recent decades, however, we are all aware of how actually existing socialism has proven neither particularly successful nor paradisaical. As a consequence, while there are a few stalwarts who continue to praise socialism—albeit an ideal

10. For a fuller account of this process, see my *Liberation Theology After the End of History*.

11. Novak, *The Catholic Ethic*, 227–28.

socialism properly distanced from anything actually tried thus far—many critics of capitalism have opted, almost by default, for at least a chastened welfare capitalism, a capitalism with a human face. And such hopes have not of late enjoyed many victories, neither are the prospects for victory particularly encouraging.

The difficulty of alternatives prompts us toward a more immediately theological or confessional critique of capitalism. The opening is provided by the phrase, "*Given* the alternatives." But what precisely, is given? Here we move from an unadorned empirical to a robustly theological argument (which, I will argue momentarily, does not surrender the empirical—to do so would leave me guilty of the crime of idealism, utopianism, et cetera). For behind the supposition of what indeed constitutes the given, the way things are, resides an eschatological claim. What has God given? What is God giving? What does our economic vision confess about God? Or conversely, what does our confession suggest about God's economy?

Christian proponents of capitalism base their advocacy on the problematic eschatological claim that in effect capitalism is the best that we can expect in this time between the times. Said differently, Christian defenses of capitalism hinge upon releasing the eschatological tension between the *already* and the *not yet* by means of emptying the *already* of any immediate material (social-political-economic) content, with the result that we are left to ponder the capitalist status-quo as the lesser evil, as the best we can expect until at some future point God decides to act. There is but one age, even as we look forward to the age to come. There is no overlap, no transformation or redemption here and now beyond the comfort offered the rich that they will be forgiven and the consolation offered the impoverished that in the next age things will be different.[12] In this barren space, where we are locked in competition and struggle for scarce resources that God has hidden (like a sadistic, cosmic Easter bunny) so that we might be prodded from lethargy to creativity, the best we can hope for is to find shelter in the shadow of

12. In defense of this claim, I offer one of the more blatant examples, from Michael Novak: "The point of the Incarnation is to respect the world as it is . . . and to disbelieve any promises that the world is now or ever will be transformed into the city of God . . . . The world is not going to become—*ever*—a kingdom of justice and love. . . . The single greatest temptation for Christians is to imagine that the salvation won by Jesus has altered the human condition" (*The Spirit of Democratic Capitalism*, 341–43). Although this may be one of the more extreme examples, Christian advocates of capitalism all share a similarly constrained account of the difference Christ makes here and now.

(depending on which theologian you consult) the state or corporation while the market manages sin according to a utilitarian logic.

The theological or confessional difficulties with this vision are legion, embracing a range of issues from anthropology to soteriology. A fuller exposition of them, however, must be deferred to another day. Now it suffices to continue the eschatological argument.

What is the alternative to capitalism? Surely the alternative is obvious. It is the Kingdom of God, where those who build, inhabit; where those who plant, harvest; and where all are filled, and the agony that currently besets us ceases. The question of alternatives is finally the eschatological one of the appearance of the Kingdom, which implies that the question of alternatives is rightly answered only confessionally. Why? Because the Kingdom is not something we build; it is something we receive. It is finally not a product of our labor, but is instead given to us as a gift. All of which is to say that the alternative to capitalism is not something that we construct, rather it is something we confess. And it is worth noting, because the Kingdom is something we confess, the rejoinder about *the best we can do* loses its punch entirely as it is revealed to be thoroughly beside the point. The interesting question never was, "What can *we* do?" but the eschatological one of "what is *God* doing?"

Here the confessional does not escape but recovers the empirical. The confession advanced against capitalism and its Christian courtiers is that the alternative to capitalism has *already* appeared, even if it is not yet present in its fullness. The ages are not juxtaposed; they overlap (1 Cor 10:11). God has given and continues to give *here and now* more than capitalism's Christian proponents can see.

What is it that they fail to see? For one thing, the way that God has and continues to gather persons together into a body called the church where, by means of the divine things in our midst—Word and sacrament, catechesis, orders, and discipline—human desire is being healed of its capitalist distortions and set free to partake of a different economic ordering, one ruled not by scarcity and struggle, debt and death, but by a charitable logic of donation, gift, and perpetual generosity. Christian proponents of capitalism fail to discern the divine economy that is already taking form in our midst as persons enter into new economic relations, giving and receiving, exchanging, not according to the rhythm of capital's axiom of production for the market but animated by the Spirit of faith, hope, and love. In more recognizably political and economic terms, this divine economy takes the form of what the Christian tradition identifies as the works of mercy. The corporal and spiritual Works constitute the beginning of God's reordering of human polity and economy in accord with the Kingdom. In other words, the works of mercy are the ecclesial instantiation of the divine economy and this economy is already taking shape in our midst in countless ways and communities—in various alternative markets and co-ops, houses of hospitality, sanctuary and jubilee movements, and gleaning projects, all of which engage in and encourage economic production and exchange according to a logic other than capitalism.

I recognize that these are fabulous claims, especially for readers (like myself) who have been so thoroughly disciplined by capitalist economy and theology. But Christianity confesses a grand God who gives grand gifts. Nevertheless, it should be said that when rightly understood and practiced, the works of mercy are not susceptible to the charge of being an instance of mere charity, that is, of being an example of the modern hobby of philanthropy that contributes a few percentage points of one's disposable income to worthy causes while ignoring broader systemic issues (what liberationists call *structural sin or injustice*). On the contrary, the Church's practice of the works of mercy corresponds with the best insights of the liberationists. For example, it takes little imagination to see the correlation between various elements of the works of mercy and what liberationists call *integral liberation*. The works of mercy are holistic in breadth, addressing sin and the rupture of communion in its personal, social, and spiritual dimensions. Moreover, the works of mercy are not synonymous with romantic notions of personalistic politics that seek change by means of individual, one-on-one acts of kindness to the exclusion of systemic concerns and communal efforts. Indeed, such a misunderstanding is symptomatic of the way that tradition has been eroded by the acids of modernity, which has little place for a public, political Church and as a result has consigned the works of mercy to individuals. Yet as they have been practiced across the ages, the works of mercy are a corporate activity. They describe the struggle for justice and liberation of a people, of a public and therefore political body named the Church. In this regard it is worth noting that no less than Adam Smith recognized the economic potency of the Church's practice of the works of mercy when he wrote the *The Wealth of Nations*. There he noted that the hospitality and charity of the church were very great, maintaining the poor of every kingdom, and he laments that those practices "not only gave [the church] the command of a great temporal force, but increased very much the weight of their spiritual weapons."[13] Indeed, he goes on to observe that the Church constituted the most formidable obstacle to the civil order, liberty, and happiness that the free market could provide. But alas, he is glad to report that eventually improvements in "arts, manufactures, and commerce" not only conquered the great barons but undercut the Church as well, weakening both its spiritual and temporal authority by rendering its charity merely economic, that is, more sparing and restrained.

Conclusion

By way of conclusion, I want to return briefly to the difficulty that the question of alternatives poses. Why is this? And why does the confessional critique and proposal I have begun to advance here feel so eccentric, so thoroughly lacking in persuasive power? Because, I fear, too many Christian critics of capitalism actually share the confessional weaknesses of capitalism's proponents. Too many do not think that God is doing a new thing—establishing a new economy—through the ecclesial practice of the works of mercy. Too many critics share the anemic eschatological vision of capitalism's Christian proponents. God is not doing a new thing and certainly not through the Church. So the question of alternatives remains, what is the best that *we* can do? Marx or Smith? Against this dim eschatological horizon, opposition to capitalism is valiant, even heroic, but finally futile, tragic, and therefore culpable. If the options are between two secular economies (secular in the sense of the starkly human power that finally moves them, not in the sense that either are lacking in religious justifications) and if the options are Marx or Smith, then I fear that capitalism's proponents are right, capital may be the best we can do. Stubborn idealism notwithstanding, we humans have certainly not shown ourselves capable of the Pelagian task of fulfilling the promise of (Marxist) socialism.[14]

But alas, we are not alone or abandoned, even temporally, by God to make the best of the scarce resources we can accumulate. To the contrary, even here and now in the midst of the descending darkness of capital, we

13. Smith, *An Inquiry into the Nature and Causes*, 5.1.3.3.

14. I am careful to qualify my dismissal of socialism this way because there are supernatural forms of socialism—by which I do not mean Christianized Marxist socialism—that avoid this critique and actually comport with my constructive argument. See, for example, Milbank, *Being Reconciled*, 162–86; and Long, *Divine Economy*.

have at our fingertips—as close as bread and wine—all that we need to resist until Christ comes in final victory. So as the prophet Isaiah says, we are not trapped in an economy that does not satisfy. In other words, we are not all capitalists, even now.

chapter 13

Theology and Capitalism
An Interview with John Milbank

by Ben Suriano

The Other Journal (*TOJ*): In our journal we have featured several theologians and their critiques of capitalism, and Daniel Bell's article discussed how capitalism can't really be judged empirically, that is, it can't be judged on whether or not it works, because it may work all too well according to its vision of the good. You've made a similar point against the Frankfurt critique of capitalism as irrational, when in fact, according to its own contingent, ontological construal, it can be very rational. So I was wondering then if you could start out by laying out some of the salient problems with the rationality of capitalism; despite its alleged efficiency, how might it be a bad thing and how might we even say that it is irrational?

John Milbank (**JM**): Yes, that's a very interesting question. I agree with what Bell said, and I think that one issue here is that the Marxist critique of capitalism tended to be seen as manifestly irrational, in other words, as conflicting with the mass of basic human needs. There is a certain sense in which that may be true, but it ignores the question of what ends you actually elect, and that concerns questions about what ends you decide are desirable and worthy to pursue. There is more of an ethical question involved here than what Marxism tended to admit—in other words supposing everyone goes along with the idea that there is this endless kind of agonistic competition in the marketplace [that functions] according to a set of rules and [that] this means that if you play the game, you can possibly win. Even if you're at the bottom of the pile, you can possibly win. But there are going to be an awful lot of losers.

Now, it seems to me that it's possible that people kind of fall in love with this game, if you like to put it that way, and there is a sense in which that's not necessarily irrational; but purely from the point of view of most religious ethical visions, this seems to be a fundamentally false option. And I think it's possible to point out that what's being pursued here are sort of singularly empty, abstract kinds of ends—simply you're piling up a kind of nominal wealth, and then if you have a lot of this nominal wealth, you are accorded respect. To some degree it allows you to have the goods you want, but it also allows you to have, if you're successful, far more than anybody could really need. And above all, it gives rather more control over this accumulation of abstract power; fundamentally what it's delivering is this kind of nominal power in a sort of gigantic fiction that everybody is simply going along with. And I suppose in that sense, you might say that it's irrational because reason, or a practical reason, would surely opt for some particular substantive goal rather than simply a kind of empty goal. In other words, there is something nihilistic, I think, about capitalism.

And nihilism is not necessarily irrational, but it's the rational denial of the ultimacy of reason, because in the end, if there is nothing, there isn't even reason. I think capitalism is deeply aligned with nihilism, in that kind of way, that if you're insisting that we need to pursue substantive ends, what Marxists calls *use value*, yes, there's a sense in which capitalism is irrational. But I think that the problem with Marxism is that use value is not as transparent as it tended to think, that we can have different accounts of what is useful or most useful or most worthy of human pursuit.

TOJ: Could you speak a little bit on the genealogy as far as the theological origins that you see—the heretical theology that you see as conducive to the sprouting of capitalism?

JM: Yes, I think [that capitalism] has several origins. I think, first of all, perhaps [in] extremely pessimistic strands of Augustinianism—[strands that are] not true to Augustine himself, but [that are] within the Protestant Reformation and within the Counter-Reformation, where you tend to despair altogether of human activity in this world—you just see it as the realm of Satan. So you come to the conclusion that the best you can do [in this world] is some sort of very efficient regular organization but as it were disciplined vice by vice. You get this sort of thing said quite explicitly within certain Lutheran writers, for example, and it's a sort of very one-sided view of something that Augustine had to say—and I think it's echoed today in the views of those premillenarian evangelicals who think there is no way at all in which you can build toward the coming of the Kingdom.

Again, this somehow just hands over the secular sphere to sin and the idea [of] this sort of system of disciplining sin by sin. And it's striking that if you look in the early nineteenth century, often the most enthusiastic celebrations of the market are in fact evangelical, both in England and the United States, that they tend to see the market mechanism quite literally as a providential mechanism, [although] maybe more secularized, like Adam Smith, who saw it half-heartedly as a providential mechanism. [. . . I]t becomes quite explicitly a providential mechanism but, again, it is a way of disciplining sin, and [it] also is a way of rewarding those who work hard in this world and in a disciplined fashion, and it becomes something like a sign of election. And it's extraordinary how distorted this system is, that you get [the system] and these sort of success-orientated evangelical villages now permeating Latin America and Africa as well as the United States; and this question of why there is a symbiosis between a particular kind of theology on the one hand and the market on the other hand is, I think, a very, very crucial issue.

I think another theological root of [capitalism] is an over-stress on the individual and [a] downplaying of the significance of the church as the Body of Christ, as a community. And that can often go along with a stress on the idea that the crucial thing about the individual is his or her will, that God is thought of as supremely possessing an absolute will, and then He accords certain rights to individuals who are supremely characterized by the possession of the will. And then you think of these individuals as coming together and contracting together, and you get a very unreal picture of society as built on [a] contract between individuals. But I think it's linked to a very unreal picture of the will as being a kind of pure act of choice rather than a kind of tendency of human desire that's always linked to reason.

So I think another thing that feeds into this is a sort of element of a natural theology in the eighteenth-century sense, where you're trying to read off of the hidden hand of God's design in the social world—you need the divine in nature, and you get the divine in the social world. And it's again the idea that God's design is shown in the way [that He somehow] coordinates the desires in individuals and in the way that He produces good out of bad. And the trouble is that bad here is often seen as necessary, a kind of ontologization of evil and of violence.

111

TOJ: And this is where you claim that political economy became a theodicy.

JM: Yes. Theodicy is one of the roots, in fact, of political economy. I think that's very much the case. It comes to a head with somebody like Thomas Malthus. And so what you're seeing often in the evangelical embrace of the market is a strange blend of elements, [such as a] theodicy that comes from a natural theological discourse [but is then mixed] with the natural tendency [. . .] of sociology [to base itself in the laws] of the market, where the unnecessary and inevitable price for everything is determined in a mechanical way [. . .] by the supposed laws of supply and demand. I think you'd have to get an impression of the idea that people form society—it's not [. . .] completely planned; it's the result of a lot of very long-term, habitual tendencies—but that's not the same as saying [that] the social up-shot is the accidental outcome of the unconscious matching of supply and demand that's going on. In fact, the market doesn't really work like that at all; it works rather through a systematic and semi-deliberate economy of desire that's deliberately engineered by social forces.

TOJ: We will have to flesh out your thoughts on the market or on the economy and how that possibly can be regulated from certain substantive visions of the good. Before we do move on to that, I would like to ask you to maybe flesh out a little bit more—how evangelicalism is complicit with this sort of perverse theology and the market in general. How does it celebrate the market? If, as you have said, evangelicalism is centered on an individualist practical reason and also has "kitsch-laden content," which is very much a part of marketing strategies and very much a part of legitimating and perpetuating capitalism, what are some very outstanding examples of this today in, say, American evangelicalism?

JM: Well, I don't know an enormous amount about it, but I think that nowadays, almost deliberately even, mission and evangelism are thought of in market terms of maximizing your product and that people will talk even of grace as being a commodity quite explicitly in the so-called free market theologies. But you mentioned that this is kitsch, and I do think that is quite important because it is a tendency to see mediation as some-how dispensable, so that an analogy can be made here with the idea of the commodity, that capitalism is not interested in the product. The product is just a given, and then it's a question of how you sell it.

Obviously, in terms of religion, there is an interest in the product, but somehow the product is regarded in this very systematic way. You have a kind of bundle of doctrines that people tend to think they clearly understand. And you have a kind of literalism at the theological level and an insufficient sense of mystery that God is an absolute mystery and that we grasp Him at best very, very, very partially. And I think that if I insist that our grasp of God is partial and inadequate, you realize that the knowledge we do have of God is already mediated, and that the way in which we transmit that knowledge, or the way in which we enact that knowledge liturgically, is a continuing part of that mediation that affects the very concept of this religious knowledge—so that aesthetic considerations are central, I think. But if you have banal modes of preaching or you use banal images or dreadful metaphors about car engines and that kind of thing, you're actually betraying the content of what you're talking about.

TOJ: Definitely.

JM: It's because the medium is the message, as Marshall McLuhan put it, who not accidentally was a Catholic. And obviously I'm not saying this is true of all of the American Protestant tradition, it's obviously not. And you know the very greatest thinkers, like Jonathan Edwards, did just the opposite; they made aesthetics the heart of what they were thinking about. But [. . .] the culture of the megachurch and the very anti-urban culture—people who really prefer to live in a kind of no-man's-land of shopping malls and that sort of thing—they're suspicious of downtown because it's too corrupt, and they're happy all the time with banal restaurants, fast-food, very bland kind of architecture. And to my mind this betrays the Gospel, because I think how we treat space and time is central; the whole business of sacred time and sacred landscape is essential. And one of the things I've noticed strongly in America is that, I believe, up to the middle of the twentieth century, America was a sacred landscape in that I think it had its own quite austere but very beautiful aesthetic in its modes of building and things. And that very rapidly in the last part of the twentieth century, the rows of strip malls and that sort of thing have produced the most incredible uglification of the landscape; and in my mind I see this as spiritual deterioration—profound deterioration—and it seems to me that the kind of religion that is at ease with that is a very strange kind of religion, because it's not really thinking about how we are trustees of God's land and that the beauty of the creation is the divine call to us, that the divine demands from us an adequate response.

You know, there's a sense in which the whole business of human beings is to worship and glorify God. Indeed, this is Calvinism, proper Calvinism; our business is to glorify God, is to worship God properly, and that has to extend through every aspect of life. And I think it's no good having a dualism where you're kind of worshiping God on Sundays when you're supposedly leading a very proper goody-goody family lifestyle, but outside that you're behaving rapaciously, without concerns for the neighbor.

TOJ: Yes, definitely.

JM: That's what worries me.

TOJ: It's a privatized type of religion that is very concerned with the development of the soul, but as far as excluding or objectifying certain social relationships outside of it, that's not much of a problem or an impingement on it.

JM: Yes, but you know you can't develop your soul properly if you're not concerned for all the relationships that you're in—

TOJ: Exactly; the two are inextricably linked.

JM: Precisely.

TOJ: Well, I was wondering if you could now discuss the church as the Body of Christ; and before we take up this idea of stewardship in making the public space more beautiful, trying to rectify some of the spiritual deterioration that you speak of. How do we understand the Body of Christ in a more beautiful vision, in a more beautiful economic vision and a practice that might be able to counter some of these tendencies?

JM: I think we've only just begun to think about this. But I think that the Body of Christ is Saint Paul's image, and I do think that in Saint Paul the economy of grace and the real economy are really linked with each other, and the church essentially is a community of gifts; it's a community that is rooted in the Eucharist and in the reception of the life of God. And I think that when Paul characterizes the life of the church as a constant exchange of material gifts but also gifts in the sense of talents, he insists these are for the up-building of the body. It seems to me that somehow what we fail often to think through is that grace is also material practice—or the mediation of grace is also a material practice—so that we're constantly supposed to be bestowing grace on each other and our social relations are supposed to go beyond simply duty or what is demanded toward always doing something extra; but this is mutual, so it's not a completely disinterested thing; it sort of goes beyond the contrast of disinterest and interest.

And I think this is why sometimes Paul can sound almost shockingly selfish. I think that's the point, that he's saying, well, these are my needs, and I'm supplying your needs, and these are my needs of the church here and the church there, and they have to constantly supplement each other. Then it's as if he wants to have a new kind of community that's not simply tribal, and yet it's not simply a community of law on the other hand, a community of law in the city that would go beyond the tribe. But here he is inventing something more like a super-tribe, where the bonds are more familial and passive and not simply legal and political bonds, so that ecclesia is, if you like, the invention of a global community. And it does include an economic dimension, and I think that the key thing here is that we have to think of all exchanges in the end, though they will obviously involve contracts and money and all the rest of it, but in the end the standard is something like the exchange of gifts, a fair exchange of gifts toward a mutual up-building—even things like fair-trade practices, which [are actually] much more extensive in Europe than in America—but you can see in a way that is kind of a gift-exchange model where you're buying a product from the [developing] world that's a good product—it's organically grown—and then you're giving a fair price that allows good conditions of production and support for workers and such; you can see that, in a very small way, as an exchange of gifts. And the question is, how do we build that on the larger kind of scale? It seems to me that people are often saying this, but I think it's characteristic of Christian social thought—Catholic social thought [. . .] and some Reformed social thought as well—it tends to insist on the intermediary associations between the market and the state, in other words, on bodies that are free associations that are not simply concerned with profits and yet are not simply concerned with law.

And neither market solutions nor state solutions are what Christian social thought should be favoring but, on the contrary, entirely new modes of economico-cum-social-cum-educational practice; in other words, [. . .] small communities or interlocking communities [committed to] total formation, if you like to put it that way, where you're concerned with producing material things, but at the same time, you're trying to promote spiritual ends and ecological ends and educative ends. So in a way we need to abolish the idea that there is an economic realm, a pure, sheerly economic realm simply concerned with producing wealth. And this is an idea that very much was brought forward already in the nineteenth century in Britain by John Ruskin, the idea that the division of wealth that you get within capitalism is a false idea of wealth: it's not real wealth in the sense of real flourishing; it's something abstract, and we need an economy that's concerned with real flourishing. And I refuse to think that it's unrealistic or utopian. [. . .] I think up till recently you could say education has not been concerned simply with profit; [it] is concerned with flourishing. And why does that work? It works because people are trained in a certain way, and they're taught certain codes of honor, so that success is measured in terms of whether you're achieving these goals of flourishing. And if it's a goal that you simply try to become rich, you would lose honor, and you will probably be struck off the record—quite possibly, that could possibly happen to you—because it's not true that self-interest means here you're simply striving to be rich and powerful, because the honor of what you're involved in, which is a public thing, it's a public reckoning of honor; you will simply lose face. I think probably we need new measurements of honor [beyond our] fear of life. So it's not utopian—I'm not asking people suddenly to be altruistic, pure and simple.

TOJ: Now, it may not be utopian, but how do we deal with the complexity of just transferring this economic vision from the church to the organization of society and economy—specifically, how do we bring this into the heterogeneous, political context where we may be able to expose formal rights and market mechanisms?

JM: I don't know. I don't even know if anybody in advance will be able to work that out. I think we have to work on several fronts at once; I think we need to blur the boundaries between the church and other things. The church needs to penetrate other things, become the focus for lots of different things. Why shouldn't the church, for example, get into banking is one question; why couldn't we have church banks organized on a cooperative kind of basis? I think consumer action is one thing, and encouraging the growth of cooperatives is another [. . .] thing, but I think certain realist voices will say, "Well, yeah, but the problem is the big corporations and all those sorts of things." I think it's not stupid to work also on the business schools and on the corporations themselves; I think vestigially people always do want to do more than just produce profit, but one should always work on increasing that. It may possibly even be that the ecological crisis will present people brutally with these kind of issues, but the danger there, of course, is that you may simply get a kind of techno-scientific, capitalist solution to that as well, which could lead to a more tyrannical kind of society; but it might at least present us with a certain window of opportunity. But the real problem is, and I don't know that I have the answer to this, that in industrial capitalism there seemed to be a certain mode of activity—you had unions, you had strikes, you could work toward battling against capitalism, you could even have the idea of a revolution taking over the handles of the state. None of these models seem to be available any longer or plausible any longer, and so I'm not sure that we have a very clear plan. I can only suggest that we have to work on a multiplicity of fronts, and it just could be that at a certain point you cross a certain critical mass that has developed such that suddenly things have flipped over into something else.

TOJ: You say we don't really have certain types of labor unions or certain means of resistance available like in the past to really counter capitalism and get the ball rolling on this, but how might your understanding of the Christian socialist legacy more specifically aid in some kind of transformation?

JM: Well, as I say, I think it's so strongly linked—ideas about guilds and cooperatives, the idea that somehow you need professional associations at every level that are concerned with the quality of what's being produced and the quality of labor and not simply a matter of demanding labors. How one reinvents those kinds of notions, I'm not entirely sure. Also, I think there is a remaining role for the state—the state has set up a framework of laws that regulate of things like profits, very strict regulations to ensure that people aren't simply making money for the sake of making money, and to some extent, the organization of an education and welfare state may have a role. There is a quite interesting division here. I think sometimes in the United States of America both the left and the right are very, very suspicious of the state. In Europe there tends to be less suspicion of the state, and you probably see that even in contemporary Christian thought, that probably people in Britain who don't see the role of the state as fundamental nonetheless give it a slightly bigger role maybe than, say, someone like Dan Bell would for example. There could be that kind of distinction possibly. I mean it's still a small but a noticeable division I think.

TOJ: And that's why I wanted you to speak a little bit more about some specifics of a Christian socialist legacy. Because in America—especially in forms of evangelical Christianity, as we spoke about earlier—there is a very, very big suspicion of the state. And of course socialism immediately calls to mind central-state-planning socialism.

JM: Which isn't of course what it means fundamentally; the main socialist tradition was not about that but was about spontaneous cooperation and so on; rather than the intervention of the state there are Fabian social democratic traditions, Marxist traditions, and so on, but in some ways, the more mainline socialist tradition fit more with New England ideas about self-help, Jeffersonian ideas about self-help, and small-scale local organization, and so on. I think these terms are extremely slippery; I think between left-wing versions of Catholic social teaching on socialism of the cooperativist type there isn't in any sense a huge distinction at all. Another important word here is *distributism*: certainly in Britain many people who saw themselves as socialist sometimes also saw themselves as distributists—they weren't always necessarily alternative terms. Eric Gill, for example, had these artistic socialist communities; he sometimes thought of himself as socialist and other times as a distributist. Distributism places a very big stress on as wide as possible distribution of property; it savors the idea that everyone should own real material things: the house, the tools of their trade, these kinds of things.

And it goes along also with the idea that as far as possible things should be produced at a local level, a kind of Wendell Berry sort of idea—that you exchange things when that's necessary, not simply for the sake of it—and I think particularly that insofar as possible you try to be self-sufficient in agricultural production, the idea that there is something fundamental about the agricultural economy because this is the production of food and clothing and so on, the basic fundamental needs of the human body, and the materials you need for building houses; but when you get away from the idea that that is the guiding basis of the economy, you're into something decadent. I think the agrarian currents in American thought, that today would be represented by somebody like Wendell Berry or David Schindler, are very close to certain currents within European socialism of a certain kind. Of course they can be seen as romantic, but today in the face of this ecological crisis, they can also be seen as realistic. I think Wendell Berry's articles are particularly good in fact.

TOJ: Yes, he does have quite a bit to contribute, especially to our ecological crisis and how to understand that from a more agrarian level, like you say.

JM: That is not to say that all complicated technology is wrong. It's a question of the use of appropriate technologies, and the use of advanced technologies to support human flourishing and creativity, rather than to suppress them.

TOJ: Yes, yes.

JM: But I think that's a massive issue—how we stop being enslaved by technology?—that nobody has any really good answers to.

TOJ: I was wondering if we can ask a few more questions, including one that may be a question you've heard all too often. But when we speak about the ecclesia being a global community—and as we've just been talking about, trying to infuse the economy with a gift-type economy that would definitely require a substantive Christian vision of the good—how do we understand this as something other than a theocracy? And you have said before that a theocracy, a traditional notion of a theocracy, relies on the dualism between the sacral class monopolizing the divine over against the secular order. But could somebody argue that this is still a more subtle, maybe even more democratized, if you will, form of theocracy?

JM: Yes, well, actually they could. Yes, they could, and maybe it is in a certain sense; I don't know. I think the crucial point is that the power that is running the law and the system of punishments, these must not be things that are directly in the name of God, and there mustn't be certainly a quasi-sacral caste that is performing these actions in any sense at all, for all of the Augustinian reasons that this is the city of this world, and it's a secondary good, and the whole system of law and punishment is necessary because of sin and so on, and so it's quite important that that area is distinguished from the church. But when it comes to special bodies that are to do with education or the economy and so on, it's not so clear that these aren't units of the church. I mean a monastery was an economic community; it was a farming community, but it was fully part of the church and the guild organizations in the middle ages. There were also fraternal bodies that were part of the church, so, yes, in a sense I do sort of see the permeation of church into all these functions, but they're not strictly political functions or socioeconomic. So if you were to say, "Well, this is in a way a kind of democratized theocracy, a democratized, anarchic theocracy," I suppose I couldn't really deny that in the end—I guess Stanley Hauerwas would probably say something rather similar.

TOJ: And it would be a matter of really trying to expose other formal regulations and rights as themselves also adhering to some kind of metaphysical conception of the good.

JM: Well, and you said absolutely the right thing there—yes, that in a way they aren't free of theocracy, and that in the end maybe all political notions are theological notions.

TOJ: And I guess for our closing question, how do we keep our theological vision—our community that's based on a certain theological vision, in this case an economy of the gift—how do we keep that open? [You have said before that] it needs to be an exchange outside of itself with the infinite unknown; it needs to value encounter in meeting with the Other and different. How do we go about making sure it doesn't enclose back on itself, how do we keep open the possibility of encounter with something other and different within this specific Christian vision?

JM: Well, that's a very, very important question; maybe it should be part of the logic of mission itself—that you are going to receive Christ in a different way from the people you're communicating the Gospel to and also that even from right outside of Christianity you're going to receive new insights—but I guess we need to keep a sense of eschatological reserve that the church is the Body on pilgrimage, that it's never fulfilled in time—it's a process of ongoing discovery—and that we would only see the fullness of Christ when we see Christ reflected in every human person. And so this must keep [us] open to otherness. The sense of an otherness that we can't master should be at the center of the Gospel, and certainly not something tacked onto the Gospel. But I think it's a question of always discovering mediation—what William Desmond, who is a Christian philosopher, calls the sense of the "between" that is not simply respecting the other as other in a kind of Levinasian sense; it's a much more constant attempt to discover how we live with the other in a way that allows for differences and yet allows those differences to blend and coexist and so on. It's the question of a peaceful or harmonic difference that one is always struggling to bring about. But it's always true that we need the other.

chapter 14

Alida

by April Folkertsma

Go forth in peace, for you have followed the
good road. Go forth without fear, for He who
created you has made you holy, has always pro-
tected you, and loves you as a mother.

—Saint Clare of Assisi

THE RHYTHM OF her rocking body lulled the child to sleep. The night was warm, but she pulled Alida closer.

They were crouched between two wooden benches on the porch of the small train station in St. Claire, Nebraska. The station was empty and Mary was thankful. Tonight she needed to be alone with her child, to study each of Alida's eyelashes, the dimples in her elbows, the shape of her toes. Mary wanted to watch her child walk along the wooden boards of the train station and hear Alida's laughter when she chased her. Tonight she was grateful to be ignored and forgotten; tonight she had a promise to keep. She shivered and kissed her toddler.

They'd started walking in June after Alida's third birthday. Mary had planned on walking from New Orleans all the way to California. Her dream was to see the ocean before she lost her sight. It would have been a shorter trip to walk to the Atlantic, but at the convent school she'd learned that the Atlantic was known for its choppy gray water whereas Magellan had named the Pacific for being peaceful—a half-blind teenage mother needed an ocean of peace. If nothing else, the trip was a good reason to leave New Orleans and start over, like the Israelites when they left Egypt for Canaan.

Mary had been going blind since she was twelve. The nuns had sent her to a doctor when they could no longer ignore her squinting or walking into walls and knocking down icons. She'd toppled the Virgin during Mass one morning, sending the Virgin's head rolling and the baby Jesus falling out of her arms. The doctors diagnosed her with an eye disease and said the best they could do was prescribe stronger glasses. They warned she might wake up one morning with no sight at all. Now she was nearly nineteen and still able to make out the shape of her baby's nose, the blue of her eye. She had defied them all, and would have done so again by reaching the Pacific.

They'd left New Orleans with some money, a bit of food, and too many memories. The money had given out before they crossed into Tennessee. Since Alida was small and had better sight, Mary began having her raid chicken coops for eggs and gardens for vegetables. They slept under the awnings of businesses that had closed for the evening and the barns of farmers who never knew they were there. She lost her eyeglasses in such a barn when they had to scramble out the back door one morning. They'd overslept and had been woken by an old woman's broom swatting at them in the hay. Without the glasses, Mary wasn't able to go very far each day, but the truth of the matter was that the glasses wouldn't have helped much anyway. The white film that covered her brown eyes was turning the world into a gray fog.

As they walked they heard the freight trains speeding by, men offering to help them aboard. But Mary was fearful of men. She couldn't see their faces well enough to know if they could be trusted.

Instead of using the trains for transportation, the boxcars became a diversion. Mary and Alida would play games as the trains passed, singing songs to the rhythm of the passing wheels. Mary would tell Alida stories about where the trains were going, inventing lands where no one was hungry or tired, lands where people bathed in the ocean. As they walked, Alida would be her mother's eyes, helping her stay away from the tracks and the speed of the trains.

A week ago they were walking along an old road beside a sea of cornhusk green. The warm sun was burning their skin, but its brightness helped Mary to see as she tripped along the narrow road. A gentle breeze blew, and she imagined that the rustle of the corn stalks sounded the way the ocean would. Alida was holding her hand, singing, "Jesus Loves Me," her voice tinkling in the breeze like a crystal wind chime. Mary was rejoicing in a moment of pure bliss, content to be nowhere else in the world than homeless and poor with her baby girl in the middle of cornfields. She looked down to catch the glow of her child's golden head when suddenly it seemed the sun had set; the world around her had turned to night. She jerked Alida to her side, feeling down the child's body so she could pick her up. When she lifted her, they both fell with the motion, Mary unable to control her body in the dark. They sat on the road, its hot sand and stone burning through their thin clothes, and cried.

Mary's mind raced with fear. She was frozen to the spot where they'd fallen, unable to form an idea of what they should do. They had nowhere to go, nothing to eat, and no money. Hours passed. No one happened upon the road where they lay waiting.

"God," Mary cried out in her darkness, "please give me back my sight so I can find safety for my child. I promise, if you do, I'll give her back to you. Just let me find her safely to a home."

In her blindness she was able to shuffle them off the road and into a cornfield, where they fell asleep. When they woke, she knew her prayer had been answered because the first thing Mary saw was the pink curl of her daughter's ear. The sight of it was a gift; the clarity, breathtaking. It was as if her sight had been restored in a way that enabled her to see the microscopic strands of hair that stood on the edge of Alida's ear. She could even see down the tunnel of the ear which led to the two small bones where she saw the sound of the wind reverberating. Mary looked to heaven and gave thanks.

Standing, she saw a yellow church rising out of the fields. The sun shone so brightly on the old church it seemed as if the glory of God itself was beckoning to them to come and find rest in His house. She accepted the invitation and walked the path to the church. When they reached the building the door was open but no one was there. Mary gave Alida their last bite of bread. Once Alida had eaten, they fell asleep again, exhausted from the heat.

They slept through the night, and when Mary woke early morning light streamed through the church windows. Alida was whining that she was hungry and so Mary searched for food. She found crackers and wine in the cabinet under the pulpit. Communion food. Sacred food. She was hesitant to eat it, but a small voice in her head said, "This is my body, broken for you. Take and eat."

She gave some to her child and then ate a few crackers also. She put what was left in her knapsack.

Before they left she knelt at the cross hammered into the pulpit and prayed, "Christ, I will keep my promise. Once I've found Alida a place to stay, I will go. Only give me light for this road." She knew enough peace in that moment to fill the Pacific twice over.

St. Claire was the first town she came to after she'd gone blind on the road, but she'd stopped in farm towns like this before. People in these towns raised corn, pigs, and children. There would be a church on Main Street and a post office and mercantile right next door. The children of St. Claire would go to school in the one-room church when they weren't working on the farm. Trains would bring news from bigger cities, but rarely any visitors. Neighbors in these towns were family; they helped one another build barns and bring in the harvest. Mary knew that in a town like St. Claire Alida would be safe.

Mary walked down Main Street, which was lined with big maples, their colors turning for the fall. Near the end of the street was the train station. It was a small building that smelled of lumber dust and grease. It housed ticket sales and a telegraph office. A porch wrapped around the building, and benches were pushed against the walls. Everything looked as if it could use a new coat of paint. There was an open window on the east side with a ledge where tickets could be purchased. Mary walked up to the counter and rang the bell to get the manager's attention.

"Good afternoon, Miss," he said as he approached the window. Mary was already looking away from the man, not wanting him to see her eyes.

"Could I get the train schedule, please?"

"What's that, Miss?"

Mary inched closer to the window, and while looking at her feet, said, "Could you tell me the train schedule?"

"Miss, you'll have to look at me when you speak."

She did, and when he saw the white film that covered her eyes, he muttered, "Jesus, Mary, and Joseph!"

Quickly, she looked away again, and he was shamed by his outburst. She was so young, with a child. The gray of their cheeks told the story of hunger, and their tattered clothing was scarce protection from the elements.

He cleared his throat and leaned his head through the window, "Miss, what is it I can help you with?"

"I'd just like to know the train schedule."

"Ah, yes. Well, the last train leaves St. Claire at six o'clock, heading east. The next one pulls through at six o'clock tomorrow morning. Now, that one is an express. It doesn't stop, just pulls right on through on its way west." She'd been looking at the steel tracks, imagining their coolness, watching the small mirage of vapor as it lifted and evaporated into the day. "Can I get you a ticket, Miss?"

Mary shook her head and began to walk away, but he came after her. "Miss, I need to warn ya' that to ride a train without a ticket is illegal and regarded as theft." Then he bent low to her ear, "And it isn't safe for a wee child like you've got."

She looked up at him. "I won't be riding the train, sir."

He straightened himself and smiled. "Well, then, can I direct you to a boarding house for the night?"

She shook her head again and walked farther down the station porch, feeling his eyes following her.

He left for home a couple of hours later and brought her a thick piece of bread covered in saffron butter. "In case you're hungry," he said and walked away.

She hunkered down for the night, holding Alida close and watching her baby fingers pick up pieces of rock and tiny bugs. As the sun found its place in the western sky, the light of the moon cast an eerie glow through a small split rail fence meant to protect passengers from moving trains. Through the bright shadows she watched her child eat the bread and fall asleep.

Mary reached for her baby's wrist and felt the gentle thump of her pulse. She could hear Alida's deep sleeping breath and knew she would sleep for the rest of the night. She spooned herself against Alida, capturing her warmth and drawing courage from her life.

She fell asleep but woke to Alida's cries. A cool summer night wind was blowing and so she rocked the child. The moon's silver light stretched along the train tracks and beckoned her to visit. She slipped Alida out of her arms and stepped over the station fence. Jumping from the station platform and down to the gravel that formed the track bed, she landed on her knees. The rocks embedded themselves in her skin, and the sharp pain took her by surprise. Brushing off the stones, she noticed blood running down her leg. Bringing her hand to her face, she saw the traces of her life smeared there. She tasted the blood and its saltiness caused her stomach to rumble. Standing so close to the steel rails her senses were aroused and her instinct to live rose sharp and sudden from deep within her.

She scrambled back over the fence to where her baby lay sleeping. Her resolve must not be shaken, not by the beat of her child's heart or the taste of her own blood. She'd found a place of safety for Alida and now she had a promise to keep. St. Claire would gather her in its arms like a farm wife gathers chicks around her legs at feeding time. They would clothe her, school her, and feed her. When she grew up, she would marry and have a farm of her own. Mary knew this. She was certain she had found the place to leave her child. When she had traced her fingers along the letters of the town name, she felt her Pacific Ocean peace. And now she could whisper the name St. Claire in prayer as she said good-bye.

Mary looked up and studied the sky. She couldn't remember when she'd been able to see the moon so clearly. It was before she'd begun to lose her sight, but when was that? She couldn't remember anymore. This vivid gift of sight had been a blessing.

She had few hours left before the express would roll through town. She had some things she needed to do before it came. First was the note she'd written. It needed to be pinned to Alida's dress.

> *If you are reading this you have found my child. Please take care of her. She is called Alida after my mama. We walked here from New Orleans. I was hoping to see the ocean. Please tell her that her love was better than sight.*
> *—Mary den Hartig*

Then she took what remained of the communion bread from her knapsack and knelt at a bench. "Father, forgive me, and if it be possible, take this cup from me. Nevertheless, not my will but Thine be done." She ate the cracker and then sipped some of the wine she'd taken from the yellow church. Her last meal was the body and blood of Christ. She hoped it would be enough for her to see Jesus.

Tiger stripes of sunlight glowed in the east, and she knew that the train would be shooting through St. Claire soon. It was time to say good-bye. She pushed herself up from the bench and stood over Alida. She imagined how much more beautiful the child would be after she'd been bathed and fed milk and bread for a few weeks. She wanted desperately to see Alida well-fed and dressed, but she knew that even if she stayed she would never have the pleasure of such a vision. If she stayed, no one would take them in as they would an orphan girl.

Mary traced Alida's tiny lips with her thumbs and her brow with her fingers. Cupping her child's face in her hands, she captured the shape of her warmth. She wanted it to be the last thing she remembered feeling.

Leaning down she whispered, "You will be safe, and you will know peace. That will be your story to tell."

Then Mary slid her into the deep dark corner of the train station and covered her with her coat. She slipped the knapsack from around her shoulders and laid it at Alida's feet. Inside were a communion wafer and a school picture taken of Mary when she was sixteen. Shortly after it was taken, she'd learned she was pregnant.

She climbed over the fence again and jumped down to the gravel, this time landing on her feet. From the distance came the deep belly rumble of the train and a trace of smoke shaded the sky as it puffed its way toward St. Claire. Mary knelt down to the track and felt the rail shiver in anticipation. She drew a deep breath and faced the east where the sky had suddenly turned turquoise and pink. Climbing onto the track, she stood between the two rails, her heart racing.

With her back to the west, she watched the sun rise. "*Lord*," she whispered, "*you've loved me like you loved Leah with the weak eyes. You gave her children, too, because she was not loved. Thank you.*"

The train rumbled closer and the horn shook the morning sky, warning whoever stood on the rails to move. But she didn't move, and now the train was too close to stop. The ground was shaking and she could hear the gravel bouncing against the steel. Taking a deep breath, she could feel the train's smoke filling her lungs. Suddenly, warmth tingled in every part of her body, and she remembered the shape of Alida's head and the feel of her small hand. When she lost her sight she was whispering a blessing on the town of St. Claire.

chapter 15

Contraception, Consumption, and the Family Banquet

An Interview with Amy Laura Hall

by Chris Keller

The Other Journal (*TOJ*): North American evangelicals have heartily embraced reproductive technology in order to have our own biological families. What thoughts do you have on how to educate the evangelical community about the difference between being pro-family and supporting reproductive technology?

Amy Laura Hall (ALH): One way to educate evangelical Christians about reproductive technology is to consider, historically, how the nuclear family became in North America a symbol of the responsible, pure family. That occurs largely during the atomic era, during the '50s. With the return of soldiers and the creation of new suburbs, you have this sense that what is truly *the family* is two parents—and by and large the standard became two parents with only two, possibly three, children. Mainline as well as evangelical Protestants bought into that image as the icon for the best family. There are examples of this in posters that were distributed in the late '40s and early '50s by social hygiene organizations seeking to promote this vision of the comparatively independent and isolated family.

When you gain such historical perspective, you can ask a new set of questions. Is the independent nuclear family the only biblically sound depiction? You can go further to ask whether this is even the primary biblical depiction of the family. Back up into scripture and try to think through how, especially in the New Testament, Christ reconfigures the Roman family. The primary image of the family in Jesus's words (as well as in Paul's words) is the church. It is through baptism we are made heirs according to the promise. We are not foundationally related through blood ties genetically, but through blood ties Eucharistically. Through Christ, through Christ's blood, we are made one, and Paul refers to this both baptismally and Eucharistically. It is through Christ's blood that we are made one family.

When you look at those images alongside a nuclear family that is all genetically related and fairly isolated, the difference is salient. That image of the nuclear family, the four individuals—mom, dad, son, and daughter alongside the image of the Eucharistic family, calls into question our somewhat obsessive pursuit of our *own children* who will fit neatly into the Midwestern suburb.

TOJ: So stemming out of the '50s there was an elevation of the nuclear family above, at least as a Christian culture, the church?

ALH: Well, it is complicated. It is not as if prior to the 1950s you have the ideal, more biblical family. You don't have a very biblically sound version of the family in Christian history, period. But you get a particular kind of warping of the family that continues today, that is, the warping of the family as being almost exclusively about genetic and biological ties and about being primarily about the immediate, relatively small and efficient family of four.

TOJ: Recently in *Sojourners* magazine there was an article about the pro-life movement and the failure of both Democrats and Republicans to live up to their so-called commitment to the sanctity of life. The article generalized that Democrats don't support prenatal life and Republicans don't [support life] after the womb. One could infer from that that evangelicals would be guilty of not supporting a culture of life after the birth of a child in regards to their approach to health care and the death penalty. Do you agree with that assessment, and where do you see evangelicals needing to more fully embrace a pro-life ethic?

ALH: Well, this gets tricky, doesn't it? Because I know Republican evangelicals who spend a great deal of time caring for other people's children, and who spend a great deal of time teaching Sunday school. I know many conservative evangelicals who actually try to create churches that are havens, not only for children who look like their own, but other children who are neglected. I have watched Republican evangelicals actually live up to their own rhetoric that this task of hospitality shouldn't be primarily the responsibility of the government, but instead the responsibility of churches, communities, and neighborhoods. I've watched some really live up to the rhetoric, so I am hesitant to say that Republican evangelicals don't live up to the pro-life rhetoric, because I've watched some very clearly do so.

However (a *big* however), the Bush administration has been woefully inadequate in keeping up the most basic of social structures that churches and these communities rely on to do a pretty decent job on some of the most basic services like public education. While I've watched individual evangelical churches and individual evangelicals who vote Republican really try to make a difference for children in need, I do deem this administration to be woefully inadequate. They have not provided a safety net for those tasks and people who churches cannot meet.

I also think that there are liberal evangelicals who work tirelessly in public schools and in the private sector. I do deem some liberal Protestants to be woefully inadequate in the task of testifying against selective abortion, against late-term abortions, against the way individual women are choosing against birth and life. I think liberal evangelicals need to be more courageous in calling not only their Republican counterparts to task, but also in calling to task those on the left who have accepted the inevitability of a culture of death.

TOJ: In an article you wrote on the cheesy comedy *Cheaper by the Dozen* you quoted a critic saying basically that the parents in the movie are unbelievable because they are educated and successful and also have twelve kids. Given the fact that there are many children who need parents in the world, how are we to *procreate responsibly*? It feels like there is a tension there that many people need help navigating.

ALH: The whole term *responsible parenthood* is also historical, and that comes up around the '20s and '30s with the American eugenics movement, which tried to forge a distinction between responsible and appropriate family forms and irresponsible families. The argument said that with too many children one couldn't provide for them in a way that would be responsible. There was also a great deal of anti-Catholicism and blatant racism and classism going on, especially by the time you get to the '50s with this. So you have this kind of climb of the middle class trying to prove itself as responsible. You get them limiting the number of their children more and more so they can provide more material goods for their children, send more of them to college, and by and large fit the mold.

And one thing I've had people say to me is "Okay, you're critical of reproductive technology and want to try to have your own children, but also you want to call into question the meticulous timing of children that goes on with more and more effective kinds of birth control." And yes, what I see as consistent with both of those efforts—birth control and reproductive technology—is the sense that reproduction is something that one must control in order to fashion a family that will fit with one's expectations. With the onset of especially effective forms of birth control (there were ineffective forms [then] and they didn't really matter that much for how we thought about the family) and reproductive technology, you have this ever-more efficient quest of controlling one's form of family. I think this has warped the way we think about incipient life, the way we think about the gift of life, and that parenting has become so much a task.

I mean, we have become Pelagian in how we think about the gift of life. It is something that we must control, navigate, and adhere to in order to craft a family that will fit in with economic demands, that will fit in with cultural expectations. Evangelicals have to ask ourselves why: What are the norms by which we are trying to adhere to when we are seeking a particular kind of family? I suspect many of us are at least influenced by the images in the media—of Baby Gap kids, and in *Better Homes and Gardens*—as we are influenced by a scriptural witness to the gratuity of life.

TOJ: Is it wrong then to even have the approach that I shouldn't have as many kids because then I could then be more hospitable toward those children who need good parents and resources?

ALH: So are you asking should you use contraception and adopt children? Or use contraception so you could give more money to your church and tithe?

TOJ: Well, I guess I am asking both of those things, but those both seem somewhat amoral now that they have been articulated—

ALH: [*Laughs*] Well, it's not that those questions are obscene, but even as you ask such questions, to be troubled by them, I think, is to be asking the right sorts of questions. When you ask as you also simultaneously think, "ah, is that the right question to ask?" then that's the right question to ask. To ask whether or not that is the right question to ask is already doing so much more than most young couples are doing when they are thinking about having children. What they're thinking about when they are having children is crafted not by their faith but by the book *What to Expect When You're Expecting*. They're going to stick with all the rules in *What To Expect To When You're Expecting* because *What To Expect When You're Expecting* tells you that if you adhere to these rules you will have a child of the promise. That's why their little tiny section at the back of the book about the unexpected or unanticipated child with disabilities comes as such a jarring little section. Up until that point you have been reading that if you do all of these things right, you will not have the "dreaded" child, the child that is unexpected.

So what you usually have couples doing is buying these books and trying to anticipate all that they can do so that they can have a beautiful and flourishing child by all the definitions that we perceive in our society to describe a beautiful and flourishing child. That will continue your beautiful image of your flourishing beautiful family. And so even to ask questions about what images one has in view for having children goes a long way toward being more faithful. Just asking questions, why do you want to have kids? What do we have children for? A Mennonite colleague asked that right to my face at a conference—that we need to ask what are children for. He explained to the group that, in the Mennonite tradition, children are born for martyrdom. (And at that point I was thinking, that's why you're a Mennonite and I'm not.) But to even say that, to witness that in the Mennonite tradition you have children so that they can bring witness in a cruciform way to Christ's love, that's a whole different set of questions than the questions mainline evangelicals usually ask.

TOJ: Is there an approach to children in this country that seems Savior-esque, a kind of idolatry of children?

ALH: Yeah, it's a pretty surreal—Gnostic idolatry though. You get this image of a kind of disembodied child that you want. Look at the Anne Geddes pictures, an image of a child as pumpkin, or a child as flower: the baby as the commodity you get to consume or pluck and put in your vase versus the kind of images you have with Norman Rockwell. Almost all of his images of children are children with skinned knees, are of the chaos of kids. I think about the one with the boys running and trying to pull up their pants, they've been swimming in the water hole with their dog. The images of children that he depicts are children with other children, who are showing signs of mess, which children inevitably are, versus with Anne Geddes, her images are so popular—I mean all sorts of well-meaning, lovely church ladies on a regular basis put up Ann Geddes posters and calendars and use those images. And what they are is a kind of really dangerous idolatry, because you're idolizing a kind of purely platonic form of *baby*, the baby one can fashion according to one's own desires, the baby as consumable. And notice that those babies never have a sign of food on themselves; if you know anything about toddlers, you know that they are constantly covered in food. These pictures are children that do not consume; these are babies that we consume. And those icons of childhood are indicative of a dominant culture in America that sees children as a way to accessorize and fulfill one's own life, rather than as interruptions into our own hopes, dreams, and goals.

Children should ideally recalibrate our lives, and instead, we are seeking children that we can calibrate in order to fit into our hopes and dreams. That is part of why you have prenatal testing and selective abortions even among evangelical Christians. You have a real interest in sex selection and gender selection even among evangelical Christians because they have an image of what their family will look like, of what their child will look like. And there is a whole arsenal of tools now in medicine used to craft a child that will most fit. Very blessedly, the child who comes will never be a child that will adjust accordingly and be perfect in a way that you were hoping. Blessedly, even if we end up cloning someday, that child will resist merely being an image of what we want. And in that resistance I think there will be hope.

TOJ: In your interview that was published in *Christianity Today* in July, 2004, you mentioned that the crux of the technical issues about in vitro fertilization and embryonic stem cell research are more "upstream." You also mention that having genetic children and being fertile is given elevated status to caring for those who are the "least of these" and those children who need to be tended to. Where do you think Christ speaks most aptly to this problem of the objectification of the family?

ALH: Oh, the banquet, no question. Last Sunday our church read the banquet passage in Luke. No question that would be the one I would refer to. When we're going to have a banquet, what more characterizes the kind of ideal family gathering than the family dinner? If we're going to have a family dinner, who are we going to invite? Are we going to invite only those that fit or are we going to invite the children that don't fit, whether they be children who come from us biologically, the extra child that we didn't anticipate or plan and who snuck through our ever-more-efficient contraception we're using? Or are we going to invite only those who fit? I think that is a great passage for parents to dwell on.

Actually, to go even further "upstream," I think that's a great passage with which couples may start. This is something that my students get more riled up about than any other topic that I bring up. I swear, in some ways, abortion and homosexuality are less contentious among my students than the issue of what kind of wedding to have, what kind of wedding banquet to plan. The way that young Protestant couples plan their weddings bodes very ill for the kind of family they are hoping to become. You watch what a wedding is often about these days—it is about displaying one's wealth to those one is eager to impress. If you think instead about the scriptural wedding itself, about being the open banquet that one hopes one's marriage will be, I think weddings would look a lot different than they do. I think they would be on a Sunday morning service where everyone is invited. I think they would look more like a potluck than the kind of catered extravagances toward which even the middle class is climbing.

I think the image of the banquet where the blind and the lame are invited, as well as those who cannot repay us—that image would be one in which to start a marriage.

chapter 16

Dishwater, Smart Bombs, and Life Together

An Interview with Shane Claiborne

by Becky Crook, Jon Stanley, and friends

The Other Journal (*TOJ*): Shane, I'm interested in what you had to say in your book *The Irresistible Revolution* about the difference between normal and ordinary. It seems as though you make a distinction between the two, identifying normalcy as something that is not revolutionary and ordinary as something that is extraordinary. Can you explain this?

Shane Claiborne (SC): Well, the subtitle to my book is *Living as an Ordinary Radical*. The thing that I think is so important is to put those words together—ordinary and radical—because that's what I see happening all over the planet. You know, radical in the truest sense, that it means getting at the root of something[1]—getting at the root of poverty and violence, getting at the root of what it means to be Christian.

It's not a radical that's reserved just for saints and prophets. It's for ordinary folks that are doing beautiful things with their lives, and that's what I think we're seeing all over the place—folks that are, as Dr. King says, "radical nonconformists." That's where it becomes not normal to just live a life within the patterns of the world's consumption and redemptive violence and all these things that are happening in the global community.

That's what I would say is the tragedy—that Christians have become so normal in the sense that we do [. . .] sort of look like everybody else. Christians throughout history have been peculiar oddities, you know? But they're not

---

1. The word "radical" is from the Latin word *radix*, meaning root.

superhuman; they are ordinary people that have been transformed by an extraordinary God. That's what I see the Spirit doing all over the place.

I think that's why people can identify with my story. I'm not a superhuman somebody. I'm from East Tennessee. I have had a journey, and people can often find themselves somewhere along that. It gives me a lot of grace with other people too. A lot of times people ask, "Why aren't you more judgmental?" and I say, "My gosh, because I can see myself in people that frustrate me." The most troubling contradictions I recognize because I can see them in myself. I can see them in where I come from. I'm so grateful for the people who have shown me grace as a recovering East Tennessean.

TOJ: You ask a question in your book, "What do we do when we are the ones who've gone sane in a crazy world?"[2] It is striking to think that much of the way that the world is structured is actually a type of madness. You talk about being an oddity and the delightful way that what is foolish is used to show the madness of the world. Can you talk more about the idea that what seems like folly is often the deepest wisdom?

SC: Yes, well, that's the story of our faith. The scriptures say that God uses the foolish things to shame the wise, and the weak things to shame the strong. That's what God seems to be good at, and the people who God uses throughout history are not the most [. . .] noble and powerful. It's often the most subtle and the most unlikely people and places that God uses. And particularly in our world, I think that's really important.

We live in a world that uses language like *smart bombs*, and to a lot of us, they don't seem too smart (*laughs*). Maybe there's a wisdom of the cross that, as the scriptures say, "is foolishness to the wisdom of the world." The ideas of grace and love are scandalous. The way that the Amish reacted to the [West Nickel Mines School] shooting, for example—that's not people's knee-jerk reaction necessarily, but the Amish have cultivated a spirit of reconciliation and peacemaking that the world is mesmerized by.

A few friends and I are writing a book right now called *Jesus for President,* and we have a section called "The Amish for Homeland Security."[3] We ask what the world would look like if we reacted to violence in that

2. Claiborne, *The Irresistible Revolution*, 21.

3. The book has been published since the interview. See Claiborne and Haw, *Jesus for President.*

140

way. Really, it makes more sense—it's more healing; it's more redemptive. It would create a better world than what we see with this idea that violence can bring peace, and what a nightmare that is. You know?

It was Peter Maurin who said something like what you're alluding to. People would always call him crazy because he's sort of the street-preacher type. He was part of the Catholic Worker Movement and he said, "If I'm crazy, it's because I refuse to be crazy in the same way that the world has gone crazy."

It's brilliant, because if you particularly look at our world, it definitely, to many of us, looks crazy. Really, what we're doing in our community in Philadelphia is living in ways that make more sense.[4] What's crazier, spending billions of dollars on a defense shield or sharing our billions of dollars so we don't have to protect as much? [*Laughs.*]

What's crazy? And what's normal? Right now, what's normal is that the average U.S. citizen consumes something like over what 500 Africans collectively consume. Why does that seem to be normal? Why does that make sense? Why does it make sense that half of our clean drinking water is flushed down the toilet while 1.2 billion people are thirsting to death?

So our community is doing simple things, things like flushing our toilets off of dirty sink water. It's very strange, you know, but people see it and say, "It makes so much sense!" And there's something so magnetic about that.

A lot of times, the pattern we get into is so seductive that we have a sort of paralysis of imagination. But when you see something like the sink draining into the toilet, it makes sense. It makes sense to flush your poop down with dirty water. It makes sense, but we almost need permission to think outside the box.

TOJ: One of the things I appreciate is when you spoke about someone calling you on something and opening you up to a way that you could be more creative. It seems like if we're going to have imagination and accountability and open each other up to new ideas, it requires letting go of the idea that we have it all together and opening up to how we can be more creative. How do we cultivate that? How do we respond to others calling us to be accountable without being defensive and with humility? How does one become able to hear those things and respond to them?

4. The community in which Shane lives in Pennsylvania is called The Simple Way (www.thesimpleway.org).

SC: I think, first of all, that when it comes to humility, the community keeps your feet on the ground. Community keeps you accountable. You see each other at your best and at your worst. Community is good at lowering the mountains and lifting the valleys. We make sure that everyone gets celebrated in our community. And that's part of why I travel in pairs, you know—it affects the way that you share a story when someone from your community is with you. They could say, "Well, that's not really what happened" or "Well, what about this?" And so I like that accountability. I think that Jesus lived like that and said, "Go out in pairs," so that's a big part of it—being submitted to other people.

I'm thankful for people that allow me to do that and that love me unconditionally and remind me that I'm better than the worst things that I do. So community to me is also where I'm surrounded by people who are like the person I want to become. It pushes me to risk a little bit more.

As to the issue of how we're constantly changing, I'm so thankful for people that have helped me to become who I am. Whatever I am is because of other people that have opened my eyes up to what that can look like, you know, which is why it's not a strange thing to give away the money I've made on my book. You know, it just makes sense to share it with people who have been a part of that journey.

What I don't have a ton of energy for is people that just critique but don't offer any sort of constructive program. That's what I love about so much of what's happening right now is that people have alternatives. It isn't just people saying, "Don't travel," but rather people saying, "Let's be more creative than just riding a plane somewhere. Let's figure that out together."

My friend Will, who works at *Geez Magazine*, got to a conference and he was just a mess, all red and chapped, and I said, "What happened?"

And he said, "I just rode my bike 1,000 miles to get here." He didn't do that out of arrogance; he did it out of trying to do something that made sense. [*Laughs.*]

I think that type of integrity and the integrity of other people that I really respect pushes you a little further. It's also life-giving. It's life-giving to travel and stay in people's homes. It's not just that I hate hotels—although I don't like hotels much, but it's not something noble for me—staying in people's homes just gives me life. And I can't speak with any integrity if I'm going back to the Hyatt tonight. I'm not dissing other people, but I just completely get leveled and feel tongue-twisted if my needs and my ends don't meet up. I think we're trying to get there, but that's where I'm really thankful for other people who are doing creative things and inviting other people to do those things as well.

That's part of what we do—we talk about not just protesting, but "protestifying." Let's show something different if we're going to critique. Let's show an alternative.

TOJ: As I'm listening, one thing that strikes me as true, not in a super-human way, but as true in a very ordinary way that is inspiring, is how you talk about creativity. It's very energizing because all of us have the innate capacity to be creative. You are critiquing and criticizing a lot of things, but you keep coming back to the idea of cultivating imagination and finding new ways of doing things. You're not just deconstructing everything that we are doing wrong and then leaving us with a pile of rubble.

It's easy at forums and conferences that are focused around issues of justice, to come away feeling pulled down, motivated by guilt and a weighted conscience for awhile, but you seem to be steering toward a more hopeful, uplifting way of movement that is tied to imagination. And imagination is something that all of us were born with and that all of us have the ability, as people created by a creative God (if you believe that), to nurture and grow.

That's where I really hear the hope of what you're saying; you are doing some tearing down, but you're putting an imaginative structure in place, where the scaffolding might be made of something whimsical and nourishing and sustainable, instead of a resource that's quickly available but ultimately destructive. It's something different and unusual. That's the hopefulness and the ordinariness of what you seem to be saying. It's creative and yet it's also accessible to all of us.

Can you talk about these differences in motivation—guilt versus imagination—and the effects of such motivation in your experience?

SC: Well, I think that guilt is a good indicator, but it's not a good motivator. Many significant movements start with at least one sense of "Wow, that's not right. Why are we doing that?" So there's sort of a healthy conviction that comes with that, but then, that doesn't sustain any transformation or change, and it's not very magnetic or compelling I think.

What we do is more fun, and it brings me to life. At home, I get up every day and almost feel selfish sometimes that we have so much fun in our neighborhood and in what we do. Yet there are those who uphold us as though we were a sort of sacrificial people—like we've had to give up so much!

We see people coming to life in imagination everywhere. Not out of guilt, but out of a realization like "Wow, this is great! Why would I ever settle for a Porsche when I can ride a bike?" I met a guy who was saying, "Why do I drive an SUV to work and then drive it home and then drive it to work-out at a place where I pay for a membership? Why don't I just ride a bike?" And then he did.

You know, it's crazy to stay in the pattern that so many people find themselves in. We've been sold the American dream and we buy into it, and it ends up just being an empty, lonely nightmare of isolating ourselves from community and other people and imagination and life, all so that we can be the wealthiest, most miserable, medicated, depressed people in the world. [*Laughs.*]

TOJ: Bob Dylan and Bono are both figures that the Christian community, particularly the evangelical community in America, has been highly attracted to. But then, once more of a relationship develops, the community seems to kill its prophet. There's an attraction to Dylan and Bono, two people out there in the world, critiquing society and doing something different, but then at some point, the community requires that they become more mainstream—to drop what they're doing—or else it becomes death to the prophet.

Have you felt that at all or have you felt the freedom to continue to really be who you are? To be true to yourself and to your community?

SC: It seems that you're implicitly comparing me to those two figures (*laughs*). But I don't pay too much attention to all that. In fact, it was definitely a part of my Lenten journey (and I'm continuing it now) to wean myself off of anything that I'd get too narcissistic about or too absorbed in, in critique or thoughts of what people were saying.

I take what people say fairly seriously, especially when people write letters that they're angry. I tell them to call me and we'll hang out or whatever. But I've actually been amazed at how receptive people have been to their own capacity to change. I'm not claiming to be anyone's direct influence or anything. But to me, there are neat signs of humility that we're all a work in process.

I think it's important not to react to criticism in a way that is a self-fulfilling prophecy. I think Bono has a healthy number of influences around him within the church and outside of the church. It's important not to polarize ourselves, but instead we need to call each other to the best that the Spirit wants for us.

I'm really careful about that art, and it is an art, a delicate integration and balance of how much you call or push people to. Wherever we're at on a journey, a baby step is a step we celebrate. What might be really extreme for one person might be a no-brainer for someone else. But you kind of keep pushing each other a little bit or inviting people into that.

I'm really, really careful not to end up preaching to the choir, which is part of why I write with Zondervan, and I go to speak at the stewardship retreats of a megachurch. If they invite me, I'm there. I want to be engaged and not end up marginalizing myself. That's why I'm also very careful politically, definitely in how I articulate things, but also with the friendships that [I] have. I don't want to get boxed in.

So I'm careful with my language and in the circles that I would put my stamp on, you know. I think a lot of people are in that place where they're really careful with that. There are a lot of people creating a really healthy conversation and a harmony of voices without repeating patterns of political polarities and things like that.

That's part of the purpose of our book, *Jesus for President*. We want it to provoke the Christian political imagination to kind of think outside of the box on these things and to ask, "How can we have a life and witness that is radically political, but just as much radically nonpartisan and transcending a lot of the categories that we have for everything?"

I think that Jesus was not a reformist—he wasn't trying to make a better Rome. He was establishing a completely new way of living together, you know?

TOJ: In our latest issue of *The Other Journal*, we focus on *pop revolutions*. You've talked about being wary of revolutions that are commodified within a consumer-capitalist system. How do you discern that—encouraging a revolution while we live in a culture that wants to commodify revolutions?

SC: It's very tricky. There's a great book by Herbert Marcuse called *One-Dimensional Man*; it talks about how the dominant culture and pattern is able to absorb anything and that revolutions have become a sort of appendage. And so when you have thousands and thousands of protestors [. . .] show up to the Republican Convention, it only shows the power of the Republican Conventions, especially in the newsstands.

I always think that it won't be long before you can buy [Lockheed-Martin] gas masks for protests [. . .] so that everything is able to find its place and to be consumed and marketed within the larger culture. You know, the picture of the rebel sells—the picture of Che Guevara on the front of a coffee cup.

But I think that it's one of those things where you have to be wise as a serpent, innocent as a dove. For instance, there was one article about us in the *New York Times* that they called "Rebels with a Cross," and so we've had that kind of a danger for ourselves. And we've had *Time Magazine*, ABC *Nightline*, all these sleek people that want to do stories.

We're very careful about that—we discern it together and rarely do we do much of that anymore with all the hype. We're careful that we tell the story ourselves. Usually the story that they want is about this privileged group of people who have moved into a poor neighborhood and are doing all this great work for the neighborhood. And that can be very disempowering to our neighbors who have lived and survived and who are caring for each other. So we just have to be careful about that.

I think we've learned a lot from watching other groups, like Emergent. One of my critiques of Emergent would be that it's become incredibly narcissistic, and so you just end up talking about talking. It's one thing to say, "Life happens when we sit around a bar and talk theology." It's another thing to sit at a bar and talk about sitting at a bar talking about theology. You know? And so you can end up really sucking the life out of a movement.

This is why I'm not too excited to do conferences and workshops on new monasticism or the Movement, or things like that. Wendell Berry wrote a great article called "In Distrust of Movements" where he kind of gets at that; he warns not to fall in love with some big vision but to pay attention to the ingredients of it, like in *Life Together*, Dietrich Bonhoeffer says it really well. He explains that if we're in love with our vision of community, we'll destroy it, but if we really love the people around us, we'll create community.[5] That's been really important.

5. Bonhoeffer, *Life Together*, 17–39.

I've seen that in the church growth movement, where you can really rip the congregation apart trying to build your seven-point strategy for church growth. Or within a progressive, activist community, people can just tear each other apart with their vision for a better world and can be very, very aggressive and judgmental and hurtful to each other. I have seen the faces that this takes everywhere.

I wrote an article on our website in reaction to some of that. It's called "The Marketable Revolution," and it talks about the dangers of that. It's a temptation of Jesus to be culturally relevant. Most of the people I really admire within the church's history have actually called into question everything that was relevant in the culture and also many of the really ugly things that Christianity developed in the quest to be relevant to the culture.

TOJ: What you're saying about your community's effort to tell your own story and to avoid marketable hype seems to draw a parallel to Jesus's whole ministry where he doesn't want people to know that he is the Son of God. He calls himself the Son of man instead, which is a much more down-to-earth, mortal, humble title.

Many of the people that I most admire have been the reluctant prophets, the folks who had the ability to speak and articulate but didn't necessarily want to because they weren't interested in hearing the sound of their own voices or in being well known.

And so instead, the voices that get heard most frequently are the ones that, as you say, are just talking about talking. But the voices that are especially needed, it seems, are those that maybe aren't trying to be heard above the throng, but are the voices of people who are actually out moving around and doing the good work. It seems like it's also the unsafe work—doing instead of just talking.

I wonder, are you ever scared or frightened by living out and acting on this sort of radical faith, this type of Christianity that you talk about?

SC: The only thing that frightens me is when people look at us like we're saints, because I think that such an infatuation is only indicative of how far we've come from the heart of Jesus and what true Christianity has been, you know? The fact that what we're doing looks radical is an indictment on the kind of Christianity that we've become accustomed to. It's just marked by what it believes and not how it looks. That's where it's really, really dangerous.

We always try not to react to that, because on the one end you can think too highly of yourself, and on the other hand you can think too lowly of yourself, and all the time you're thinking of yourself. How do you get out of that and be freed up to do things that bring people closer to God and God's dream for the world? That's what we're working faithfully to do.

When people come up to me and say, "Man, you're awesome!" it's because they either don't know me or because they don't know God—there are lots of things that are awesome. That's the only thing that I worry about.

But for myself, I'm not really frightened of anything—it feels good to have a community and to do life together. I don't know what else to be scared of.

TOJ: Some of us are starting a community here, and something that has come up is that it seems like there is a vulnerability that is required to build very real relationships. One of my fears is how far vulnerability is extended to people you meet in the context of that community.

SC: One of my housemates and friends says [that] living in community [is] like standing before a mirror naked, because you see yourself in a very real and vulnerable way.

The community is a choice to look deeper. You laugh harder, you cry harder, you hurt each other more, because you know each other better, you know, a lot like any deep relationship—a family, a partner or someone you're married to. But you grow into that.

Community is organic—you don't jump through a lot of hoops to get there, but you grow into it. For us, we've created some things that articulate how that works pretty well, at least for us over ten years. You know, the mistakes we've made, things that have worked for us. We describe it actually organically, like an onion, you know. And so we look at the layers within our community and try to figure out what are appropriate expectations and sharing, transparency, and all that stuff that we have at each of those layers within our community.

And there are commitments that we make. When [people] visit, we don't expect them to be Christians or anything at all, really. But if people want to live with us for different amounts of time, then they make different sorts of commitments to that and we have different expectations. You know, we don't pour our whole selves out to people who are just coming for a week. Because community can also be—especially for us right now—very parasitical [when] people come and they take from your community and they leave and we end up feeling malnourished. We've had to really figure out how to do that. We've had up to twenty people a day calling that want to visit, so we do it differently now.

Part of what we do now is that we have a community every month that hosts what we call "Schools for Conversions: Learning to Live Differently,"[6] which gives exposure to a bunch of different communities all around the country. Those are all linked up to our website, and that's how we integrate other people into our community.

Some of the other things that we have that have kept constant over the years are, for instance, something that we call *straight talk*, which is the idea that you don't talk around someone, but that you talk directly to them if you're hurt or offended or if you've done something that you want to confess. We protect that. If Zach doesn't do his dishes, you don't complain to someone else, you talk to Zach about it. Talking to someone else won't resolve it anyway, you know? But we've made a commitment to do that and to protect that environment.

You know, community can also attract really broken, needy people. So we have to create a culture within it that is healing and that brings the best out of people and that doesn't do the opposite of bringing the community into one person's or everyone's unhealthiness or revolve everyone around one specific need.

We describe a lot of the things that we've [created using the image of a garden] trellis. You want enough structure within the community so that things aren't rotten on the ground, but if you have too much structure, it does the opposite of creating life and suffocates and doesn't allow things to be free and natural. It's a delicate thing.

TOJ: And does your community have a garden?

SC: Oh, yeah. We have a bunch of gardens. It's one of the places we have a lot of fun. We actually have a gardener on our block, Dominic, who we've been able to create an income for this year, so he is our part-time gardener. And we all garden together too. Actually, the Camden community across

6. Schools for Conversion, accessed at http://www.newmonasticism.org/sfc/.

the river has a big ol' greenhouse and a natural bread oven they bake pizzas and bread in, and they call themselves urban gardeners.

TOJ: In relation to gardening, you talk about the Latin meaning of the word radical, which is *radix*, meaning rootedness. What is it that most makes you feel rooted?

SC: Well, again, I think it's choosing a group of people that you decide to do life together with. That takes many different forms, but for me it helps to have roots in a neighborhood that I love. That's part of why I'm going home tomorrow morning after I just got here today (for a conference)—I love being here, but I also want to be in my neighborhood, you know.

And of course, I think growing roots into who Jesus is and trying to be those things that Jesus is. That kind of gets rooted into who we are, you know? Those are all things that I'm excited about. Those are what keep me rooted and anchored in reality.

chapter 17

Eco-Terrorism

by Paul Willis

It's true. White mushrooms
muscle up through the edges
of our new paved road.

Blackness crumbles
like the crust of tender lava
doming in the blasted
crater of Mt. St. Helens.

So long, asphalt!
You are not much, after all.

chapter 18

Theology from
the Pet Side Up

A Christian Agenda for
NOT Saving the World

by Stephen H. Webb

I HAVE A confession to make: I'm not all that interested in environmental-ism, and though I've written two books on why Christians should be more compassionate toward animals, I'm not all that enthusiastic about saving ani-mals, either. But I am interested in Augustine's insights into the unfathomable depths of original sin, so let me also confess that my confession was insincere. That is, I'm not too worried about my lack of interest in environmentalism or the rights of animals. In fact, I take some foolish pride (and here I say foolish because all pride is foolish, not mine in particular) in my skepticism about these issues.

You can blame Augustine, as well as my innate stubbornness, for my lack of passion for environmentalism. As an Augustinian Christian, I do not think it is our job to save the world from evil. More importantly, I suspect that when we try to play God, we end up doing more harm than good. Nevertheless, I do feel guilty for not doing more to alleviate the suffering of animals. Augustine, however, has helped me to see that my feelings of guilt are not necessarily a trustworthy guide to what I should do. Feelings of guilt obscure the moral clarity we need for Christ-like action in the world.

I am a college professor, so my own particular environment is decidedly un-Augustinian. Indeed, it is full of people who feel guilty about how we treat nature. Few of my colleagues go to church, but they can talk poetically about the miracle of nature and the consolations they find in the woods, streams, and mountains. All of this strikes me as a convenient way for my secular friends to justify their religious sloth, and I have no interest in making them feel more reasonable about their rationalizations.

What is more disappointing, though hardly surprising, is that many theologians have been quick to jump onboard the naturalization of the supernatural. Environmental theologians think that people can be motivated to respect nature only if they are persuaded that God is a part of nature and nature a part of God. Feminists talk about a kinder, more gentle God who gives birth to the world, and postmodernists deconstruct the rigid dualisms that they find separating God from the world. The image of an interconnected web dominates these discussions, even though that image—in spite of my name—always conjures for me a foreboding of entrapment and death.

Feminists frequently insist that the image of God as the master of nature sanctions male mastery over women, as well as nature. I have never found this argument the least bit convincing, whether it is treated as an interpretation of history or as an analysis of religious psychology. Our Christian ancestors worried about their treatment of nature only because they knew that God was in control of it, not them. If God is not absolutely in control, then nature's bounties are up for grabs. If God is the master, then we are the servants, and that image has always served to humble the human heart.

Scapegoating the Christian tradition for the consequences of the West's rapid industrialization might help some secularists feel good about not going to church on Sunday mornings, but it cannot be taken as serious theology. Again, theologians—even those who feel guilty about the way the church has flaunted its moral high ground over the centuries—should not be in the business of making non-Christians feel better about themselves.

Besides, the idea that nature is uniquely sacred hardly inspires respect for nature's otherness. If God and nature are intimately connected, then it follows that we should make nature our home as well as our church. This is precisely what has happened. Romanticizing nature as God's body only encourages people to treat it as one more item to be marketed and consumed. Think of all those people who build houses in the wild, in order to be closer to some vaguely construed source of spirituality. Think about all the billions that are spent on herbal remedies and earth-friendly products that bring a bit of nature into our homes. Environmentalists rightly worry about industrial pollution, but what do we make of all this spiritual pollution that clouds the religious landscape?

The decline of the mainline Protestant churches and the ascendancy of conservative forms of Christianity have left many people confused about the relationship of Christianity to American culture. Liberal Protestantism provided social cohesion for much of the twentieth century because it erased theological differences with the thick, broad brush of social justice. People could feel good about living in a Christian nation because the dominant form of Christianity did not offend anyone. Americans can be quite optimistic and tolerant as long as they are not expected to tolerate anything that gets in the way of their optimism, and liberal Protestantism provided the ideology that kept optimism and tolerance on intimate terms.

Conservative Christians have little tolerance for an optimism based on secular notions of rationality, and they are not optimistic that tolerance alone can provide the necessary grounds for social stability. Conservative Christians have risen to power in America largely because secular liberals no longer feel the need to have religious backing for their optimism and tolerance. Yet it is not clear that conservative Christianity can become the American civil religion of the twenty-first century in the same way that the mainline denominations were the civil religion of the twentieth century. A Christian church that tries to stand against the world has a hard time speaking to everyone in general terms that do not offend.

If my analysis of religious turmoil today is even partly correct, then it helps to explain why environmentalism has become a kind of public civil religion for many Americans. Worshipping nature, if that is not too hard a way of putting it, is an enjoyable activity that can pass as both good politics and tolerable religion. One could go further by saying that only a distorted form of religion could make the love of nature possible in the first place, because nature is, as evolutionary biology teaches us, violent, purposeless, and ever ready to sacrifice the lone individual for the glory of the species. Loving nature is a pathology born of Christian decline, which makes it a pathology that only Christianity can cure.

As I mentioned at the beginning of this essay, I was never a nature lover. I began my thinking about animals, in fact, purely by happenstance. I had a dog, a dachshund named Marie, and I loved her more than my friends thought I should have. I had just started my teaching career and my wife was in graduate school an hour and a half away, so Marie and I spent a lot of time together. To this day I cannot say that I really love all animals, or even all dogs. That level of abstraction is, I suspect, close to meaningless for anybody who is not God. But I loved Marie. I grew up with a dachshund companion, and through Marie I could smell my childhood memories. My friends were bemused, if not appalled. My lap was her throne, and when I greeted her after being apart, she would attack me with her passion. She was pure, unbounded love and gave me permission to give the same. All of this seemed to suggest something of the category of grace to me, yet our relationship, under the skeptical eyes of my friends, also struck me as terribly transgressive.

In Marie's eyes I saw the glimmer of freedom, the first movements of spirit emerging from matter, wounded by what we humans had demanded of her species. Her eyes demanded responsibility and, even more, mutuality. Howard, our cat, would only glance at me, while Marie stared. Cats have a haughtiness that makes them hard to understand. They embrace their animality in spite of their freedom. Dogs plead and thus risk losing everything. Dogs demand; cats indict and turn away. Dogs are creatures in transition, incomplete without us. To hold a dog's gaze is to set the dog free. The fragility of this dependence is easily abused, of course, but I was convinced that dogs say something not only about us but also about the origin and destiny of all animals.

I wrote my first book about animals, *On God and Dogs: A Christian Theology of Compassion for Animals,* for Marie. I was convinced at the time that loving a dog is good preparation for theology in the sense that writing about dogs risks speaking about something that is, perhaps, best left to silence. Direct speech about dogs or God sounds foolish and strained. Theologians, I suspected, write too much about the love of God, as if God is as familiar to them as their pets. We should be embarrassed by God's love, I wanted to say, just as we are embarrassed by the love of a good dog. Both loves are really too much, and both are certainly undeserving. Perhaps Georg Hegel spoke more truly than he understood when he argued that Friedrich Schleiermacher's famous definition of religion as "absolute dependence" turned the dog into the best Christian. I too wanted to write a theology for the dogs.

I probably loved Marie too much, but then again, there is something excessive in all true love. I was convinced, in fact, that excessive love is what enabled both humans and dogs to overstep their species' boundaries in the adventure that we call domestication. Domestication was not accomplished for utilitarian reasons, though such theories abound in the scholarly literature on this topic. Domestication began as a reckless venture of love that led humans to meet the eyes of the dog and led dogs to jump into the human circle. Dogs made humans out of us, just as we have gone a little way toward making honorary humans out of dogs. When Marie reached the end of her life, friends and family thought I would be inconsolable. I wasn't. I buried her in the backyard hours after she died, and I am confident that I will see her again in heaven.

I know that many of you will suspect that my relationship with Marie was more pathological than the typical environmentalist's love for nature. Nonetheless, it seems to me that loving individual animals—and loving them for what they will yet become rather than pretending that they are enough like us to merit equal consideration—is a more Christian gesture than loving nature as a whole. Ethical obligations have their origin, I suspect, with the particular and concrete rather than the general and abstract. Individuals suffer, not species. Humans and animals have a lot more in common than humans and trees. That is why I am a vegetarian but not an environmentalist. Nature is parasitical; no ethic can be drawn from its competitive and heartless strife. Ecosystems are beautiful in the abstract but shocking in their details. That we have become accustomed to celebrating nature instead of being shocked by it is an indication to me of how religiously homeless modernity has made us.

Of course, vegetarianism has its own problems, which involve, of course, the stubborn sin of pride. Vegetarianism, especially in its more legalistic form of the animal rights movement, blurs the boundaries between humans and animals. Worse, the animal rights movement is utopian (as well as Pelagian) in its optimism about our ability to change the world. Few writers make this point more eloquently than the great South African novelist J. M. Coetzee in his book *The Lives of Animals.* He raises this pointed question: Are vegetarians trying to save animals or are they trying to save themselves? That is, are they really concerned about the world, or are they trying to escape it?

In this postmodern work of metafiction, Coetzee tells the story of a novelist who holds some of the same views as Coetzee regarding the moral status of animals. The novelist, Elizabeth Costello, has been invited to give two lectures at Appleton College, where her son teaches physics. She surprises her audience by talking about the rights of animals rather than literature. Her audience is skeptical and condescending, but it is hard to pinpoint where Coetzee stands in this exchange. He has made his character old and dying, so her plea for the rights of animals can be read as a plea for herself. Moreover, she has a hostile relationship with her son and daughter-in-law, and her defense of animals further widens that gap. She also repeatedly draws the insensitive analogy between the killing of animals and the death of Jews in the Holocaust.

Costello rejects rationality as the criteria for judging animal worth, defending instead the ability of the imagination to instill sympathy. Yet Costello cannot imagine a way of healing her relationship with those who are closest to her. Her love for animals is not part of an ordered life, where everything is loved according to its place in God's creation. Instead, her love is disordered and destructive. She is scandalized by the meat-eating world, and thus she seeks not only justice but also revenge. The being of bats, she insists, is just as full as the being of humans, thereby denying the uniqueness of humanity. She can raise the value of animals only by lowering the value of humanity.

From a theological point of view, Costello needs salvation as much as the animals she defends. In the end, she breaks down, and her son takes her in his arms. "There, there," he says. "It will soon be over." This is the one moment of human contact in the story. Perhaps Coetzee is saying that only humans can worry this much about death and that human solidarity is our only defense against the suffering of others. Curiously, none of the characters mentions a personal encounter with an animal. Maybe Costello could have received the same comfort from hugging a beloved pet.

The early Christians were drawn to but finally rejected vegetarianism for two reasons. First, they wanted to distinguish themselves from Judaism, and in their missionary zeal they did not want to be hindered by dietary rules. They sensed that vegetarianism could become a new legalism that would lead to schism, something the early church could not afford. Second, Gnostic groups used vegetarianism as a means of claiming moral purity and separating themselves from the cares of this world. Gnostics did not eat meat because they thought the world was beyond the grace of God, and so they restricted their diets as one way of turning their backs on the suffering that surrounded them. Many modern day vegetarians also seem to use this commendable diet as a way of claiming moral superiority and expressing a deep alienation from the world. Somehow, Christians need to find a way of talking about vegetarianism that would not lapse into legalism or utopianism.

This is hard to do. To lapse into confession again, I should note that I was the cofounder of a web organization, the Christian Vegetarian Association (CVA)[1] that has had much success in raising the issue of diet among Christians. The point of the organization, I thought, was to provide an alternative to the rigidity and utopianism of the animal rights movement, as well as to demonstrate that New Age spirituality was not the only religious path to a healthier diet. My cofounder went on to other projects, and my new co-chair took the lead in making the CVA a leader in religious activism for animals. Unfortunately, activism and reflection are often at odds with each other. When I wrote an essay where I confessed (there I go again!) that I eat meat occasionally, my co-chair organized a coup. The CVA, it turns out, could not tolerate a chair who was not religiously vegetarian—or a chair whose religious motivation for vegetarianism did not lead to moral absolutes.

Getting kicked out of my own organization only confirmed for me that Christianity was right to value vegetarianism in monasteries and on fast days but not to require it for everyone. For Christianity, compassion should be rooted not in dogmatic claims about the equality of humans and animals or in an escapist flight from the realities of this world, but in our ability to be compassionate, to reach out and care for another being. Loving a dog, to return to my relationship with Marie, would not be a bad way to begin and practice that compassion. Until the church can articulate an alternative to the modern animal rights movement, Coetzee's story demonstrates that the Gnostic version of vegetarianism is still very much alive and well.

Unfortunately, theologians are often too hurried to talk about nature these days, and thus, they do not take the time to reflect about the nature that is closest to them—their pets. Environmentalists lift up the values of interdependence and holism, which they adopt from ecology, but these principles are another way of saying that ecosystems do not care about individuals. Rather than interdependence, I seek to emphasize relationships. Interdependence suggests that nature works quite well on its own accord, and human intervention inevitably upsets the balance. When I think of interdependence, I think of a spider's web, not a mutual affirmation of difference and dignity.

---

1. See Christianveg.com.

Christians have no business promulgating the aesthetic appreciation of coherence—a part of the whole is good as long as it contributes something to that whole—which reflects the old idea that this is the best of all possible worlds. The world is fallen, and nature is not what God intended it to be. The violence of nature is not all our fault, either, because the world into which Adam and Eve were expelled was already at odds with the peaceable harmony of Eden. If nature is fallen and its fall preceded our own, then there is little we can do to change nature in any dramatic way. Yet we can, like Noah with his ark, save a few fellow creatures from suffering as we try to warn others about God's impending judgment.

In *On God and Dogs* and *Good Eating*, I defined pets as animals who share with us a relationship of mutuality and reciprocity. So defined, they can serve as a paradigm for our treatment of all animals and even nature in general. Most people who have read this claim in my books greet it with a mixture of amazement and disdain. By beginning with a set of assumptions different from the environmental movement, my position, influenced by and yet also a challenge to the animal rights movement, is bound to be controversial and provocative to most people who currently write about religion and the natural world. If nature is fallen, yet our destiny is not completely separable from nature, and all suffering will be redeemed in the end, then animals need redemption as much as we do. We cannot turn our backs on the animal world and pretend that it would be a good place if only we were not there. Animals and humans are tied together in this world and, I want to add, in the world to come.

Nature cannot be a source of Christian morality, but it can be an object of Christian compassion. Yet it is impossible to have empathy for all of the animals that must become meals for others. Such sacrifices are biologically necessary, and to mourn necessity is foolishness. Perhaps this is why so many people today admire wild, carnivorous animals. It is easier to admire predators than their victims when there is nothing that we can do to change the one and save the other. Besides, wild animals strike us as something inassimilable to human measure, caring not for our help or sentiment. These animals follow their nature in beautiful, effortless, and dignified ways, so that our inability to make moral judgments about them tempts us to romanticize them instead. The Christian idea that God sides with the victims somehow gets lost when we watch nature documentaries, wincing but marveling at a fearsome display of power that seems innocent and natural.

Beginning a theology of the environment by reflecting on pets leads to a very different place than beginning a theology with nature in general or with wild animals who have their freedom threatened by human population growth. The nature that God pronounced good in the Genesis creation account was not the nature that forced humans to toil for their food and animals to fight each other. Animals were named by Adam, which suggests that the authority of humanity over animals is not incompatible with intimacy and friendship. Animals are meant to stand in relation with God by being in relation with humanity. In his science fiction novel, *Perelandra*, C. S. Lewis describes a planet where the fall has not (yet) occurred. He portrays the animals as both mysterious and gentle, living according to their own laws but also welcoming human company.

Traditionally, Christian theology portrays heaven as a garden, not a wild jungle, a place, like the original Garden of Eden, where God allows life to grow without the countless sacrifices of violent death. It is thus possible to argue that pets are the paradigm for the destiny of all animal life. In other words, according to the Christian teaching, animals were originally domesticated, in the sense of being nonviolent and being in a positive relationship with us, and they will be so again.

That is a radical and wild idea, but for anyone who has ever loved a dog, it will make perfectly good sense.

chapter 19

Tracks

by Jim Churchill-Dicks

This lapsed Catholic, lapsed Oregon native,
is sometimes hungry for the ground.
I pad my hand into the ashes
of an old growth pine
to paint a cross upon my forehead.

Soft in my hand, a silken
powder, there is dignity
in the aroma of what these
trees have become.

Beside my hand print, I notice a feather
and scores of tracks, osprey tracks in the ashes,
little peace signs freckling the landscape

pungent with resurrection.

chapter 20

Disciplining Borat

by Paul Jaussen

ON A RECENT trip to New York, I spotted a public safety poster on the subway. It read something like "There are 16 million eyes in New York City, and we are counting on all of them." The moral was relatively straightforward: watch for the unusual, the strange, or the potentially dangerous and report it. Less obvious was the identity of that mysterious "we." Was it the Metro Transit Authority? The New York City Police Department? The Department of Homeland Security? Perhaps it was the collective *we*, the imaginary singularity that is a place like New York? But whoever may be "counting on" us is ultimately unimportant, for the principle is clear to anyone who has ever caught a bus, walked through a crowd, attended school, or braved the public eye in countless other ways. We know how we ought to conduct ourselves, and we know that everyone is watching to make sure we behave.

As a film which takes perverse pleasure in flaunting those rules of public behavior, it isn't surprising, then, that one of the first scenes in *Borat: Cultural Learnings of America for Make Benefit Glorious Nation of Kazakhstan* takes place on a New York City subway. Sacha Baron Cohen plays Borat, a reporter from Kazakhstan who is unfamiliar with the implicit rules governing American public behavior. Throughout the film, Cohen thrusts himself upon unsuspecting Americans, men and women with no script, no sense that they're in a satiric faux documentary. The results vary from the humorous to the violent. In the subway scene, for instance, his obtrusive kisses of introduction are met with stern rebuff.

Why is everyone so uncomfortable? To be sure, there is the inescapable imposition of the garrulous Kazakh, and there's the odd fact that he is seeking to acquaint himself with perfect strangers. But Borat's presence seems to disrupt his fellow passengers at a more fundamental level. One possible explanation is that the riders, whether consciously or not, recognize that Borat violates the unspoken standard of subway behavior. He crosses the invisible yet undeniably powerful line separating the acceptable from the un-.

One of French philosopher Michel Foucault's most famous concepts, the disciplinary mechanism, precisely describes this cultural phenomenon. Simply put, Foucault claims that one of the crucial changes that brought about modern society is power shifted from centralized, absolute, and concrete places (like the sovereign or the pope) to society itself as an invisible but ever-present discipline. Think of the difference between a mob of unruly toddlers, kept in check by physical barriers and caretakers, and a class of high school students, shaped by years of standing in line, taking their turns, not talking with their mouths full. The twelfth graders are, we would say, disciplined—they keep one another individually and collectively in check. There is no need for physical barriers or a powerful monarch because the power has been diffused and internalized. This internalized self-discipline also offers privileges: the eighteen-year-olds are now granted the status of citizens, and they are able to participate freely in society as responsible adults. According to Foucault, this is the (dark) underside of the Enlightenment citizen. Only because discipline took the place of raw force could we have free society; only through the diffusion of these mechanisms could liberty emerge as a discourse and practice. Since modern freedom is in fact the product of personalized and individualized control, there is a tendency in modern society to deny discipline, to make it invisible, in order to maintain the illusion of liberty. Or so goes Foucault's story.

It could just as easily be Cohen's story. For if there is any genius behind his Borat, it is that he violates America's disciplinary mechanisms in such a way that we can no longer deny that they exist. By breaking through these hidden structures, Cohen reveals their power and omnipresence. Perhaps the most telling revelations come when Borat forces those he meets to admit that one of the unspoken American rules of behavior is to be culturally sensitive. In those moments, cultural pluralism, that marker of a free Western democracy, is shown to be a *disciplined* behavior, not an expression of liberated good will.

My general impression is that much of the buzz surrounding *Borat*, particularly from commentators with a penchant for liberal fussiness, is that the film is some sort of indictment of America's cultural bigotry and isolationism.[1] But such a reading misses the point. Whether he knows it or not, Cohen is revealing a much larger problem; he is uncovering the embedded cultural forces that maintain good behavior in the face of bad behavior, forces that create the contradictory situation in which good behavior must tolerate bad behavior. Christopher Hitchens, in his *Slate* magazine article on the film, points out that, if anything, Cohen reveals how incredibly accommodating Americans can be. He is partially right. It is more accurate to say that Cohen reveals how accommodation is itself a product of discipline—and the problem of discipline, like ideology, is that you know not what you do. If cultural accommodation turns out to be a mechanism of control, then maybe such liberal good will is not liberal, nor good, nor, for that matter, willed.

Even as it unearths the disciplined roots of tolerance, the film also makes it clear that discipline only goes so far. After a few minutes with the Kazakh reporter, a good deal of cultural sensitivity disappears. When Borat attends a meeting of the Veteran Feminists of America in New York, keeps calling one of the members "Pussycat," and claims that a scientist from Kazakhstan has proven that women's brains are smaller than men's, the feminists have no problem telling him that he's wrong. Neither does the Society for the Prevention of Cruelty to Animals employee think twice before informing him that worshiping an eagle is idolatry. The southern hostess doesn't hesitate to call the sheriff when Borat invites a black prostitute to her dinner party. And we viewers don't have problems squirming in horror when we see him throwing dollar bills at a pair of cockroaches who he thinks are his shape-shifting Jewish hosts.[2] Any one of these scenes could be the most offensive part of the film, and, inevitably, something in it will offend everyone.

---

1. To me, this interpretation is best exemplified by the rodeo promoter who tells Borat to cut his mustache because the stache makes him look like a terrorist. This same promoter later tells him that *we* (the ubiquitous, again) are trying to get gays hung. Or maybe by the white frat boys who tell Borat that minorities in this country have it made. Or perhaps the antique-shop owner who sells bumper stickers promoting secession.

2. The anti-Semitism, ironic though it may be coming from a Jewish comedian, is horrific, as others have pointed out. But so is the bigotry against "gypsies," which few people note, not to mention the cracks about women, the disabled, the residents of Uzbekistan, et cetera. One of the effects of so much offensive behavior is to reveal a hierarchy of value; we realize that we see some offenses as worse than others without any apparent reason. It may be fine to joke about one people group, but we cannot make the same cracks about another.

The question is, will we recognize ourselves in that offended sensibility? Part of Cohen's strategy, it seems, is to never leave anyone a way out, even as he buffers the universal culpability with humor.[3] It is too easy, and I would say dishonest, to watch the film from the perspective of pure condemnation, waxing moral superiority with a statement along the lines of "Americans (or Southerners, or Texans, or New Yorkers, or Pentecostals— pick your other) are such racists, bigots, hypocrites, fascists, materialists, et cetera, et cetera!" For then we fail to see that it is our vices and follies, hidden beneath a cultural mask of tolerance, that are on display. Foucault's disciplinary mechanisms have the strange effect of letting us off the hook; they keep us from seeing what we actually believe, act like, feel, and what we will not tolerate. At its most basic level, then, Borat cuts right to the heart of what it means to be a product of culture, any culture, whether Kazakh, British, American, or subway. In that respect, *Borat* may be a more radical interrogation than its fans or foes suspect.

---

3. And sometimes, though rarely, apolitical humor. The naked wrestling scene is pure MTV *Jackass* ridiculousness; it is funny if you can handle it, revolting if you can't. But it's almost a relief compared to the unbearable discomfort that so much of the film provokes.

chapter 21

Nine Alive!

(Newspaper headline. Somerset, PA)

by Marjorie Maddox

This is the popular miracle
to which we bow down,
a gasp in our throats,
thousands ready to weep,
disbelief exhaling relief
and not that dark mine of tragedy
that keeps collapsing
around this tunnel of a country.

But there are other wonders too:
untelevised, deeper down,
the tap-tap-tapping
left between breaths
hungry for spirit—
that canary not-yet-dead
in our damp labyrinth—
the way we long for light,
for even a candle-glow of joy
for what was once lost.
"Alive! Still Alive!"
our pulse mutters,
trying to pray.

chapter 22

Sex, Sacrament,
and Community

An Interview with Lauren Winner

by April Folkertsma

The Other Journal (*TOJ*): In your book *Real Sex: The Naked Truth about Chastity*, you say, "Without a robust account of the Christian vision of sex within marriage, the Christian insistence that unmarried folks refrain from sex just doesn't make sense."[1] What is a robust account of the Christian vision of sex? How can we talk about sex in a more Christian way? And, as you yourself ask in your book, what does our belief that sex belongs in marriage teach us about what good married sex looks like?

Lauren Winner (LW): People often don't like it when I say this, but good married sex is allowed to be ordinary. Premarital sex derives its seeming thrills from instability, from the unavoidable uncertainties of non-marriage relationships. There is nothing ordinary about non-marital sex; it has no normal qualities. When you are sleeping with a guy you just picked up at a bar, you are not bringing your whole self to him; you inevitably dissemble, hiding the fact that you had a lousy week at work, hiding the fact that your sister screamed at you and you are fragile. In marital sex, we are allowed to bring our whole (messy, broken) selves into the bedroom.

TOJ: How we live out our sexual lives cannot be a private affair, it affects community and needs to be part of a larger community conversation. Could you define what community is and what private life is? If sex belongs in marriage, what role do marriage and sex play in the Christian community? And how can the discussion of sex become part of the larger community conversation?

1. Winner, *Real Sex*, 25.

LW: In the Christian grammar, very little is private. Some things might be personal, but very little (if anything) is truly private. When we are baptized, we are opening up the whole of our selves and our lives to the church—we are allowing our very body to be knitted into the body of Christ. So categories of experience that secular America has defined as private—how we spend money, how we have sex, how we inhabit time, for example—these are categories that are no longer ours but are part and parcel of our living in community.

One of the many experiences America has privatized is marriage; we believe that marriage is something given to two people for their companionship, fulfillment, happiness, and perhaps for the rearing of children. While companionship, kids, et cetera, are clearly part of marriage, in the Christian landscape I think we have to see that marriage is not given exclusively, or even primarily, to the couple. (And insofar as it is given to them, it is for their transformation, not their fulfillment.) It is given to *the community*—the church—to be a sign to the community of God's relentless faithfulness. Other people's marriages instruct me in what faithfulness looks like.

TOJ: Both you and Wendell Berry discuss the idea of sex outside of marriage as merely a distorted imitation of sex. When intercourse is portrayed in movies, TV, or other media such as pornography, it becomes only what an artist, director, or screenwriter interprets it to be. So often, then, media defines for the rest of us what is erotic. Can you help to describe erotic and also what happens when the erotic becomes a commodity? Have we turned *erotic* into an idea about individual pleasure and therefore don't have a healthy view of what erotic is?

LW: Yes, we've done just that. Think of how many movies depict sex, and then think of how many movies depict sex between married couples. Most depict sex between unmarried people, or between people who are married to other people. Pop culture gives us very few pictures of what sex looks like between a couple that has been married for five years, or fifteen years, or thirty-five years.

So the pictures and scripts we have in our head are of decidedly unordinary sex. We learn from these images to equate eroticism with newness.

TOJ: In your book, you discuss the idea of chastity as something [other] than merely saving sex for marriage. Can you discuss this and include in this discussion the idea that one of the church's only resources employed to discourage premarital sex and sin is guilt? The result of this is that when one doesn't feel guilty, they continue to have sex or indulge in sins of their choice. What resources should the church or communities be using to encourage chastity?

LW: For starters, we don't always feel guilty when we sin. Our feelings are broken and fallen, distorted by sin, and thus not consistently in touch with what is really real. Hence, sometimes we do something that is sinful, that is bad for us, and we don't feel bad. So, for that reason (as well as other reasons) guilt trips are not great ways to keep people on the straight and narrow.

Further, Jesus did not run around guilt-tripping people. He described for them the kingdom of God and invited them into it. And he also described the consequences of saying no to that invitation. I think we can model all of our discipleship—not just discussions of sex and chastity—on that. Start with a positive presentation of what is good and true about the Christian story of sex, talk about how this is good news, and then also discuss what the *no* to this good news looks like.

When I speak to college students about sex, for example, I always include a discussion of the ways my years of premarital sex misshaped how I understand sex. Two years into my marriage, I still have to unlearn the idea that something has to be new and uncertain to be sexy; I am still learning what it looks like for stability and real intimacy to be sexy. But I also always discuss the promises of forgiveness and repentance. To talk about the effect of sinful behavior without proclaiming loudly that God forgives sin is patently unbiblical. Further, it is, in my view, always important to underscore that virginity is not the litmus test of sexual sinlessness. Though I certainly believe that one who, like me, marries after having sex has something to mourn, it is also important to recall that by Jesus's standard—the standard of lust—every one of us has sexual sin and sexual brokenness to deal with.

TOJ: In understanding sex as being not merely about my own individual pleasure, what about masturbation? Is there a place for it in community?

LW: This is actually something I changed my mind about when I wrote *Real Sex*. When I started the book, my basic approach to masturbation was to think that the evangelical community was too obsessed with stamping it out. And I still think, to some extent, that's true. Masturbation, or the lack thereof, is not the end-all be-all of Christian sexual ethics. But when one asks a question about formation—what is this act, masturbation, teaching me about sex? What sexual stories is it giving me?—the selfishness and individualism of masturbation is clear. If sex is about a total self-giving to the other, and about being totally received by the other, well, masturbation isn't sex. And habitual masturbation is destructive because it teaches us that sex is all about our pleasure whenever we want it; again, that's an understanding of sex that is in deep tension with the realities and joys of marital sex.

TOJ: Describe how sex is incarnate, sacramental, and other-directed.

LW: It seems to me that how sex is incarnate is sort of obvious. It is this thing we do with our incarnate bodies. (That sex is incarnate is one reason porn is a problem. Porn is faux sex with a computer screen, with an image, not with a real person.) As for sacramental and other-directed, Christian tradition has historically articulated three *ends* of conjugal sex: sex unites, [it] is procreative, and [it is] sacramental. That means, in simpler language, that sex is meant to unite two people, it is meant to lead to children, and it is meant to recall, and even reenact, the promise that God makes to us and that we make to one another in the marriage vow—that is, we promise one another fidelity, and God's Spirit promises a presence that will uphold us in our radical and crazy pledge of lifelong faithfulness.

Each of these three ends of sex has a basis in scripture—that sex unites is hinted at in Genesis 2:23, when Adam says that Eve is "bone of my bone, flesh of my flesh." The sacramental end of sex is hinted at in Ephesians 5:32, when Paul, having offered a set of guidelines for how husbands and wives should relate to one another, says, "This is a profound mystery—but I am talking about Christ and the church."

At first blush, it seems like something of a non sequitur. But in fact, it tells us what marriage, and marital sex, is: a small patch of experience that gives us our best glimpse of the radical fidelity and intimacy of God and the church. Finally, procreation is spelled out in Genesis, too, in God's instruction to be fruitful and multiply.

Sex's procreative ends help us understand what sex is about. The point is not just that we make babies as a way of propagating the species. Openness to procreation means that sex is hospitable. It is open to the interruption of another—of a child. Without a quality of hospitality, sex can become too inward focused, too two-people-gazing-so-intensely-at-each-other; the openness to procreation is part of what helps sex not become, in Kierkegaard's phrase, "an ingrown toenail." Procreation is not the only way for sex and marriage to be hospitable—it would be absurd, for example, to suggest that an infertile couple or married seventy-year-olds shouldn't have sex because their sex could not be open to procreation. But without the openness to procreation, couples may have to be more differently intentional about making their marriages hospitable to others.

This returns us to the sacramental. All of the Christian sacraments eventually redirect us away from the sacramental moment itself and back to the church and the world. We don't, for example, get baptized so that we can then just hang around with other baptized folks. We take the grace and transformation we've received and share it with the world. We don't come to the Eucharistic table, receive the Eucharist, and then sit at the table preening with other communicants. We take our Eucharistic grace and go back to the world. Similarly, we do not come to marriage simply to hang out with our beloved, but to take whatever grace and transformation marriage may offer us and then offer it back to the world.

TOJ: How do love, sex, and marriage reveal God's grace?

LW: Contemporary pop culture tells us that sex is always extraordinary. It is always about swinging from the chandeliers, extreme sports goes to the bedroom. "Great sex," as defined by *Cosmo* and *Maxim*, is threatened by ordinary domestic practices; it is threatened by the household, by the dishes in the sink, by the kids down the hall.

Christians ought to be critiquing this vision. Household practices are one channel through which Christians come to embody the Christian virtues of mutual care, forgiveness, generosity, community, interdependence, and reconciliation. Our humanity cannot be separated from the sorts of practices that are distinctly human: the moments of joy, anger, friendship, sadness, attention, confusion, tedium, and wonder that unfold over time and in specific places. Human intimacy is hammered out on an anvil made of nothing more than ordinary household practices. Love, sex, and marriage, to be theological, must drink from the very same wells. Love, sex, and marriage, to partake in their transcendent mission of encountering God's grace, must attune themselves and embrace life's decidedly untranscendent daily-goings-on.

In a Christian landscape, sex is indeed tremendously important but not because each and every sex act is an act of emotional intercommunion. To the contrary, what's important about sex is nurtured when we allow sex to be ordinary. This does not mean that sex will not be meaningful. Its meaning, instead, will partake in the variety of meanings that ordinary life offers. Sex needs to be clumsy. It should at times feel awkward. It should be an act we engage in for comfort. It should also be allowed to hold any number of anxieties—the sorts of anxieties, for instance, we might feel about our child's progress in school or our ability to provide sustenance for our family. Sex becomes another way of two people realistically engaging the strengths and foibles of each other.

Sexual intercourse is not only transformed as we allow it to take on the varieties of the commonplace, but the varieties of the commonplace themselves are transformed, as well. We might better understand that human love is forged in, say, time spent cooking together, or in picking up our loved one's laundry, or in spending time calming our children's fears. By opening up sexuality to these sources of our existence, we are doing nothing more than opening up sexuality to the sources of human love. Through sexual practice, we come to find each other fallible, and we come to love each other for the way we watch each other create very human lives out of those very fallibilities.

This gets back to the question of community. The sorts of challenges that attend creating community—all of which revolve around the complexities of being responsible to the other—are present in our sexual lives. The stuff of creating community—which we experience as work, as at times more than we can bear, as taking an extraordinary amount of time, and as requiring that we make ourselves present to the other—is the stuff of creating a Christian sexuality. To say that marriage ought not be a personal endeavor is to say more than that Christian marriage is transformed into a communal endeavor by exposing the deep inner workings of our marriages to members of our communities. Instead, we need to expose the deep inner workings of our communities to our marriages; we need to take what we know about being a community and bring it to bear on sex.

chapter 23

There Is Only One Thing

by Joel Hartse

WE POP-CULTURE-engaged Christians love to claim things as our own. From *The Matrix* to *The Simpsons* to Radiohead, if it's not altogether evil—if it's at least "vaguely Jesusy," to use Anne Lamott's phrase—we will somehow squeeze and twist a thing until it is almost Christian.

So let me be the first to claim the Canadian pop band Stars as my favorite drug-using, sex-having, love-promoting, totally non-Christian Christian band ever. They may be too hedonistic, poppy, sentimental, political, and occasionally just goofy. But we cannot write this band off for a simple reason: a sincere and exhilarating love radiates from everything Stars puts out. And it's all kinds of love: sexual, spiritual, platonic, even something approaching that elusive agape.

The band's very name should give us a clue: they are not *the* Stars. As Torquil Campbell sometimes reminds the band's audiences, "We are stars and so are you." This is more literal than figurative: Anglican priest and scientist John Polkinghorne, in *Quarks, Chaos, and Christianity*, reminds us that "every atom of carbon inside our bodies was once inside a star. We are all made from the ashes of dead stars."[1] There's more to this oneness of humanity than just our physical makeup, and Stars sings about it all: the big stuff like sex and death and smaller details like high-school reunions and shared taxi rides.

The band is in the habit of beginning albums with thesis statement-like epigraphs. Their first LP, *Nightsongs*, begins with a spoken quote from the poet Charles-Pierre Baudelaire's "Invitation to the Voyage," which is translated "all is order and beauty, luxury, peace, and pleasure." *Nightsongs* was sexy and hungover, an album about looking for love in bars, deserted city streets, and painful memories. There's an electro-pop slickness to the album and its successor, the *Comeback* EP.

1. Polkinghorne, *Quarks, Chaos, and Christianity*, 21.

The 2002 album *Heart* starts with each band member earnestly stating his or her intentions: "I am (name), and this is my Heart." The first track, "What the Snowball Learned about Love," is a tender song about a curious cat watching its owners make love. The whole record is wonderfully alive to the possibilities of romance, its apex being the soaring "Elevator Love Letter," a joyous assurance that there's something much better—the arms of the beloved—waiting for the downtrodden file clerk at the end of the day.

Set Yourself on Fire, which was released in the United States on March 8, 2005, starts with a more dramatic pronouncement: "When there's nothing left to burn, you have to set yourself on fire." This sets up a grander vision for Stars and concretizes the manifesto of what the band calls "the Soft Revolution," which, I daresay, is something we Christians might do well to be a part of. The personal is the political, goes the old progressive slogan, and on *Set Yourself on Fire* it is difficult to separate the personal from the political, or for that matter, the religious from the political, the sexual from the religious, or the infinitesimal from the infinite. This is not to say that Stars thrives on contraries; their philosophy is more all-encompassing (remember that carbon) than paradoxical.

The best distillation of the album may be the title track, which is partly a reference to the practice of Buddhist self-immolation, a suicidal gesture which, as Charles Orzech writes in his essay "Provoked Suicide," is "meant as a creative, constructive, and salvific act [. . .] intended to remake the world for the better of everyone in it."[2] The title can also be a metaphorical call to become fully awake and alive to the possibilities of life and love—like the way evangelical Christians talk about being on fire for the Lord.

The repeated mantra of the chorus, "there is only one THING" (emphasis in the original liner notes), over a frenetic, driving bass line, then, can easily be taken as a reference to a mystical monism: the song is a litany of people, places, and things; from "a cancer ward where the patients sit / waiting patiently to die" to "inside your lover's head," all is one.

But I must confess I hear something a little less Buddhist in these lines. In my head, the idea expressed in this chorus goes on for much longer: I follow "there is only one thing" with something like "only one thing that matters, anyway, and that one thing is Love, and that Love is

2. Orzech, "Provoked Suicide," 137–60.

embodied in Christ, and Christ's Love envelops and sustains us, and we should reflect that same Love to envelop and sustain one another."

The rest of the album, too, is full of love, and it spills out everywhere.

Most of the songs feel like small miracles, from the tired sensuality of "Sleep Tonight" to the subdued celebration of "Calendar Girl." "Ageless Beauty" may be Stars's tightest pop song yet, and it is characteristically bursting with hope: Amy Millan sings "We will always be a light" (again, my brain continues, "... for hope, love, joy, peace, patience, truth, justice, Christ ...") and asks the listener to "loosen your heart." "What I'm Trying to Say" is sweet without being saccharine: what I'm trying to say, as it turns out, is simply "I love you."

Nobody is gentle and loving all the time, of course, and "He Lied about Death" is a downright vicious attack on George W. Bush ("I hope your drunken daughters are gay," hiss Millan and Campbell). But why do they hate the president? Certainly because of his war, but also, notably, what Campbell and Millan perceive as his replacement of love with fear. "You scared the love out of here," they chastise. The best revenge in this case, though, is living more musically. The song closes with a blistering, screeching, two-minute instrumental section that is as danceable as it is angry. Frustrated by the seeming impotence of political protest, Stars opts to simply make music in the face of fascism and oppression.

What is the Soft Revolution, then? The lyrics to "The Soft Revolution" offer clues, and in them again are echoes of the Gospel. "We won't let the sun go down / we'll chase the demons out of town," Campbell promises. "We are here to make you feel / it terrifies you but it's real." I can't help but think of John 10:10, in which Jesus says, "I am come that they might have life, and that they might have it more abundantly."

Stars is no more a Christian band than, say, the Beatles or Aerosmith, but when I listen to them, my heartstrings vibrate. This is why I will keep recommending their music to people who care about the things I believe God cares about, the things Christ teaches. I will warn them that they'll be wading through drugs and sex and death and war and hate on these records, but what they'll find at the end is hope, faith, and always love.

chapter 24

The Nation-State Project, Schizophrenic Globalization, and the Eucharist

An Interview with William T. Cavanaugh

by Ben Suriano

The Other Journal (*TOJ*): Much of your work is an attempt to trace the genealogy of the nation-state, searching out its arbitrary moments and constitutive myths. What are some of the dominant myths that you see currently continuing in legitimating the state's power and how it maps social relations today?

William Cavanaugh (WC): I think one of the primary myths is the myth of freedom and openness: the idea that what we are essentially about in liberal democracy is freedom to believe and do what you want within certain bounds. It is a myth of an essential respect for the diversity of ultimate projects and ultimate meta-narratives, as if the state imposes none on the body politic but allows for all kinds of meta-narratives to be free. This emphasis on openness, then, leads to an imperative to share that openness precisely because we begin to think of ourselves as the universal subject who has transcended all particularity. Then this project becomes infinitely exportable and expandable to other societies.

Herein, I think there is a real link between freedom and violence in that way. That is, we find it imperative to share the blessings of this openness and freedom with others because we see ourselves as the universal subjects, yet this self-image is only such by repressing its own and others' particularity. One significant example of how this myth of the state has taken hold is in the idea of America as the "reluctant super power": this idea suggests that America reluctantly has had greatness foisted upon it in the twentieth century by responding to particularities like communism and fascism through a transcending of such into total openness. Yet I think this myth pertains not only to America, but is really imbedded within the whole liberal project in a way.

Moreover, the whole myth of religion and violence as inherently linked really dovetails with this as well. Acting as the universal subject who has transcended particularity, we come to think of our own violence as occluded by the idea that we have supposedly overcome violence defined as particularity. This then assumes that it is only the holding on to particularity that causes violence through its refusal of the state-endorsed universal, with religion being a primary form of such particularity: it is as if people clinging to their particular religious beliefs, which are not judicable within the eyes of the state project, is what really causes violence.

The answer to this understanding of violence therefore becomes an attempt to overcome blind particularity, most often thought to be represented by religions, in the direction of the inclusive and neutral universality of the state. As a result, we have this kind of false innocence about us, as if we are the most peace-loving and open of societies because we are beyond particular attachments. This myth is one of the ways that a country like the United States, with a military which is bigger than all the other militaries in the world combined, convinces itself that it, in fact, is the most peace-loving of countries.

TOJ: You have mentioned in your work Charles Tilley's idea that the process of state building is a process of war making, almost like organized crime, in trying to centralize this power and these loyalties. And the centralized ordering of social space now seems to be more de-ritualized and secularized without the older particular loyalties of the past. Yet you have claimed in your work that in order for the state to develop this seemingly open, secular order it nevertheless uses quasi-religious liturgical practices that are somewhat of a religious parody in order to discipline and instrumentalize the devotion and imagination of the people. Can you comment on this movement of de-ritualizing and yet using quasi liturgies by the state in order to gain allegiance and order? And what are ways it is still apparent in the United States?

WC: This process of state building and secularization is a very ambivalent movement because it certainly is the case that the liturgical rhythms of previous societies have been truly washed away. This is evident in the ways that the rhythms of time have been changed. Sundays used to be days of rest, and now everything is open all the time on Sunday and everything is available 24/7 on the internet and so on, which really does de-liturgize society in a way.

But there are exceptions to this. I think the primary exception is the way that rituals of national patriotism are highly symbolic and highly ritualized and liturgized, especially as they revolve around the flag as the central totem symbol. Here I really like and refer to Carolyn Marvin and David Ingle's book, *Blood Sacrifice of the Nation*, where they give very graphic evidence of the way the flag is treated as a sacred object. And it's really [Émile] Durkheim's theory that is elaborated in a vivid way regarding all the rituals that surround the flag—for instance how it is not to touch the ground and how it is to be buried when it is done rather than simply thrown out. These measures, therefore, indicate its sacredness and as Marvin and Ingle argue, the flag is also a central totem that organizes sacrifice, particularly a sacrifice around war.

This can be seen in Ken Burns's recent series on World War II, where those whom he interviewed portrayed a nostalgia for that era of common purpose where everything was organized around the ritual sacrifice of going to war. And this patriotism, expressed in its loyalty to the flag that calls upon sacrifice for war, is not a merely peripheral sort of engagement. Rather, as Marvin says, what's true in a society is what is worth killing for. Therefore, this kind of sacrifice is a sacrifice that produces truth for the society as it upholds the state project as the highest, most sacred reality and organizes the energies of the people according to such. That is the primary way I see liturgy still manifested.

TOJ: Globalization seems ostensibly, in contrast to the state project, to open up a more universal order beyond the hegemony of the state and its forms of pseudo-universality in nationalism, possibly offering more opportunities for worldwide communion. Yet you claim that globalization does have its own peculiar and problematic logic for configuring social relations. Could you discuss this logic or this mode of organizing social relations and how it might still be in collusion with the state project?

WC: Yes, well, it does offer up a more universal order—I think there is no question about that. The question is whether it produces communion or not? There is indeed a sense in which there are good things about globalization, as it does facilitate some kind of communication between far-flung places of the globe. Increasing the means of communication can potentially be a good thing, so I don't want to make blanket statements about globalization as if it is all bad.

But the way globalization is often manifested and dominantly played out is through a claim to hyper-universalization. In this sense it is just a hyperextension of the project of the state, which, as we discussed above, is itself a type of movement toward universalization over and against local forms of community.

Therefore, the same movement is at root for both. And any such project of repressing and sacrificing the particular for the universal does not really lend itself to true communion. True communion has an emphasis on the particular as well as the universal: it is a way of seeing the image of God in the other and yet being able to relate to the person not as a kind of interchangeable part for something else, but as irreducibly particular. Both identity and otherness have to be preserved for true communion. John Zizioulas's new book, *Communion and Otherness*, is a wonderful Trinitarian reflection on this.

The idea of universalization is, however, an ideology that is true for some and not true for others. This is because capital moves freely across borders now but labor does not—this is one of the key places where class analysis should not be ignored. In other words, what is globalization for capital is not globalization for labor. If you think of globalization in terms of moving plants to Mexico, in that sense it depends upon the border which separates Mexico from the United States such that one mile south of the border you can pay someone fifty cents an hour and one mile north of the border you may have to pay them seven or eight dollars an hour. Globalization therefore really depends upon nation-state borders in order for capital to have the ability to seek out the cheapest labor in any part of the globe while labor remains unable to be as mobile. So on the basis of this complicity with national borders, the idea that globalization is just the overcoming of the nation-states I think is untrue. I think that has to be looked at much more carefully.

TOJ: With this complicity between the nation-state and globalization, what then do you see as the shared quasi-theological anthropology that is more deeply engrained within each? What do they both assume about the nature and purpose of humanity?

WC: If I had to put it in a nutshell, I would probably say it's the denial of death, or that is, the transcendence of death and particularity. This emphasis on freedom and universality is in the most basic biblical sense an attempt to "eat of this and you will be gods." When it is at its worst, of course, it is the kind of primordial sin of Genesis 3. Again, there are many good aspects of this kind of universality. For example, there are good things from having access to the internet. You can have access to a lot of things that are good things and have communication with a lot of people in good ways through this kind of hyper-mobility.

In discussing the perverse character of globalization I don't want to ignore these good aspects because any doubts about globalization are easily caricatured as some sort of Amish-Luddite sectarian anxiety from someone who does not consistently use indoor plumbing and that sort of thing. Therefore, I don't want to say there is nothing good in it, but at its worst what underlies it is an attempt to transcend our particularity and transcend death, and that's the most fundamental problem.

TOJ: You have mentioned in your works something of the "schizophrenic character" of globalization, which has also been commented on by many others such as [Jacques] Lacan, [Gilles] Deleuze, and [Fredric] Jameson in different ways to name a few. I was wondering if you could expand on how you understand its schizophrenic character?

WC: I have a feeling that the word *schizophrenic* is probably being used in a way that's not very faithful to its original meaning if you were to look it up in the *Physicians Desk Reference*. But what I mean, if I am to use that term, may be best illustrated in the following: there is this stretch of road near where I grew up, in a town that used to be surrounded by cornfields, which has now spread west and is surrounded by shopping malls and subdivisions and so on. This one stretch of road fascinates me every time I go past it. It's right in the middle of an Illinois cornfield, and there is a McDonald's restaurant that has been recently built in the style of the original ones from the 1950s. Next to that is a restaurant with a medieval

English castle theme and next to that is a seafood restaurant with pirate paraphernalia, and next to that is a fast-food Mexican restaurant with an eighteenth-century Spanish mission theme. It is all utterly fake, and it puts us in this really weird situation where I don't even know if you could discern what an authentic suburban Illinois culture actually is. Instead we've got [it] available to us [at] all times and all places [. . . .]

You can have anything you want from around the world or any time you want—you can just storm right into any place or time. Yet we are everywhere and nowhere at the same time. There is, then, this tremendous sense of nothingness and nowhere-ness. It is as if, when you are standing in front of this strip of road you could just as easily be in Quebec or Sidney or Bangkok. So you are in a way everywhere and nowhere; you're every time and no time at the same time, which leaves no identity except for the identity of pure difference. And this, ironically of course, produces not real difference but conformity. You could be anywhere and there is still a tremendous homogeneity. You could drive coast to coast for three thousand miles and pass this same scene repeatedly. This is, then, what I think of as the schizophrenic type of character—it is this doing away with identity for the sake of pure difference and yet the difference itself is not real difference at all.

TOJ: What other social pathologies might this system require or perpetuate?

WC: Well, it produces detachment from people. I do a talk where I discuss detachment from production, because we don't make anything any more; from producers, because we don't see the people who make them; and consequently from products themselves, which rounds out the three forms of detachment now so prominent. That is, consumerism is not an attachment to things but a detachment from them and a disposability of them.

Along with this detachment, there is a certain kind of pathology, a mode or way of *seeing* space and time. It is a universal gaze that I have noticed in my students at a university where there is an assumption of this universal gaze. This is prevalent, of course, in what we tell our students all the time: that we are going to take them from their little provincial small towns in Minnesota, and we are going to give them the world and make them universal subjects of the university. It is amazing the way they assume this character and assume their ability to enter into any time and/or space.

We teach a course on the church in Latin America and we used to start with Rigoberta Menchú's autobiography. It is incredible how quickly these suburban middle-class Minnesota kids assume that they can identify with this Guatemalan peasant woman. And the message, of course, if we are going to be honest, is that who we really identify with in the story are the landowners who cheat the peasants. But they assume that they can really just walk into the story and immediately identify with this Guatemalan peasant woman. So in light of this presumed gaze, I want to give (God knows nobody will ever allow me to do this) a commencement speech at a college where I would stand up and say, "Please don't go out and change the world. The world has had enough of well-meaning middle-class university graduates from the United States going out and trying to change the world and the world is dying because of it . . . go home. Go home to your little towns and work in your father's hardware store. I beg you." That's really what I want to say.

TOJ: So you mentioned this pathological character as a mode of seeing. Our last issue was on the phenomena of pop revolutions and the wide array of revolutionary images and symbols and practices being disseminated on the market. Can you comment on how this form of seeing is in collusion with the market parodies that we now have of revolutionary images—which seem to be now an almost complete commodification of the category itself of revolution?

WC: Yes. Obviously, I want to change the world in one sense, as I am a Christian, and I am therefore in favor of revolution. I think Genesis makes Jews and Christians revolutionaries right from the start. The whole idea of the fall means that the way things are is not the way things are supposed to be, and so there is a revolutionary principle set up right from the beginning. Therefore, clearly I think that revolution is an imperative in that sense. But the problem is that revolution just cannot be made by sheer difference—it cannot be made by saying "not this" and "not that." But often what is assumed to be revolutionary in our society is really at base this kind of destruction of and relativization of everything, as if any form of authority is wrong and to be doubted and everything is disposable. But it is impossible to make true revolution out of that. There has to be something positive and not just destructive.

The problem with a lot of the students I encounter who want change is that they are not revolutionary because nothing sticks. You just cannot get any traction when everything is disposable. In order to be a revolutionary, you have to start from a particularity—you have to start from a particular place and have a very particular vision and not just a vision of generalized change. I teach different kinds of students, and there is a large Catholic studies program here on campus where the students tend to be fairly politically conservative, although not across the board by any means. But I think there is more revolutionary potential in those kinds of students who have a sense of the seriousness of life rather than other kinds of students who posture themselves to be more revolutionary because they're detached, and yet nothing sticks. With these latter students there is no way to get any traction with them because everything is merely somebody's opinion.

TOJ: And so, then, you're mentioning that we need to take on particular identities, substantive identities and practices and narratives in order to truly see in a certain way?

WC: Yes, but not just any identity will do. There are plenty of particular identities that are demonic. There is nothing good per se about particularity. But I am thinking of the Christian narrative and the particularity of Jesus Christ and to understand and perform this well, of course, there has to be this interplay of unity and otherness at the same time. So I don't want to say that particularity as such is in and of itself a good thing, because obviously you can point to Nazi Germany and talk about blood and soil and that sort of thing, but there is nothing good about that.

TOJ: So then, how do we conceive of the universal and the particular, how do we find a site or location or a form of practice? More specifically, you have done much work on exploring and understanding the Eucharist as another way of seeing and imagining and mapping social relations—so how do we understand the Eucharist in a revolutionary way or as an alternative to these other forces?

WC: Yes, well I don't want to say that the Eucharist in and of itself is a kind of panacea, as if there is an automatic nature to it or anything. But the Eucharist is the material participation in God's redemption of the creation. And I think that if it is understood and practiced rightly that it can overcome these dichotomies of global/local and me/you and God/human and identity/otherness, et cetera. All of those dichotomies are reworked and transformed in different ways.

I have talked about the way the Eucharist in particular overcomes the dichotomy of local and global. This is because, on the one hand, it is something that is cosmic; it's the body of Christ and it unites people from all over the globe, and on the other hand, at the same time, it is intensely local because it is a gathering around the communion table in one particular place. So there is a kind of particularity there, but it is also invites everybody regardless of age, class, gender to gather around the table. So, yes, I think that if it is understood and practiced well it can help to heal a lot of these dichotomies.

TOJ: How can we understand it being practiced more explicitly as a political act? How do we understand the Eucharist as affecting change at a structural level without it being reduced to just another political cause or form of identity politics?

WC: Yes, well, the Eucharist doesn't do anything. God does things. Sometimes we lapse into the idea that the Eucharist does this or the Eucharist does that. But I think it would be a real mistake to try and politicize the Eucharist and politicize the liturgy in a direct way and do liturgies for Burma or liturgies against global warming and so forth. I think that's a real danger.

I think it is better to see the liturgy and the church as a politic in and of itself, as a way of organizing and symbolizing and relating to the world—and specifically in a way that overcomes sacred/secular dichotomies so that we don't have to make it relevant by introducing something from an alien field, as, say, the field of politics. The liturgy itself imagines the world as God sees it and returns it to God in thanksgiving and praise. There was never any kind of pure nature or natural way of seeing that could instruct the Eucharist, from outside of its own vision, on how to be politicized for other causes.

TOJ: What are some ways that you have seen the Eucharist commodified? Especially in speaking of the attempt to politicize it, would you consider something like the U2charist to fall into that category?

WC: Yes, goodness, this can be a problem. But I don't want to criticize it too much, and I do like U2. I think the danger is in shaping the agenda of the Eucharist rather than letting it shape us. And yes, it can certainly easily be commodified if we see it as something that we can shape and manipulate.

One of the wonderful things about belonging to a boring church where all of the rubrics are set is that it kind of frees me up from having to tinker with it and make it relevant. Certainly there is room for different kinds of music and I am in favor of various modes of enculturation in certain forms of culture. But in general, the idea is that God shapes us in the Eucharist, and it is not that we have to tinker with it in order to make God say or do what we want God to say or do. One of the wonderful things about the Eucharist is that it turns the act of consumption inside out. Instead of just consuming something, God consumes us. It is the idea that we are made into the Body of Christ by eating the body of Christ, which is this weird sort of turning the act of consumption inside out.

TOJ: Could you give some concrete examples of communities or organizations that you think are carrying out a Eucharistic vision?

WC: I give a number of concrete examples in my forthcoming book, *Being Consumed* (how's that for a shameless plug?).[1] Examples range from community-supported agriculture to fair trade to the Focolare Movement's *Economy of Communion.*[2] It's all about breaking down the perceived boundaries between what is mine and what is yours.

1. *Being Consumed* has been published since the interview.

2. See the Economy of Communion website at http://www.edc-online.org/index .php/en/.

chapter 25

Going Out

by Debra Rienstra

When Martha heard that Jesus was coming, she
went out to meet him, but Mary stayed at home.
—John 11:20

The tomb's black jaw
cored and crushed me, too.
But see, my heap of brittle bones
rises up to crawling,
puts on a shred of flesh,
goes out.
Sometimes hope is in the hands and knees,
even when the heart lies still.

If I had thought it through,
If he had been there,
If I had spoken—
Well, this I know:
A scattering of ifs clutters the heart
like dishes and scraps left after a meal.
I will not let this rest,
even now.

Faith pushes on in the pace,
in the rhythm, small and slow,
like a broom, sweeping, sweeping.
I will try his mercy as I might.

Does not the goat give her sweet milk
only when we draw it out?
Does not the water lie still in the well
unless we pull, pull, with aching back?
Our mother Rebecca—did she not rise up
and carve a blessing for Israel?
Then I will say,
"Even now, Lord."

Some say I press too hard on the yoke.
Let it be so; I cannot wait and weep.
He is tender to the patient, silent, helpless;
but Jacob's daughter stirs his glory—
even I,
going out to meet him.

Bibliography

Bell, Daniel M. Jr. *Liberation Theology After the End of History: The Refusal to Cease Suffering.* Radical Orthodoxy Series. New York: Routledge, 2001.

Benne, Robert. *The Ethic of Democratic Capitalism.* Philadelphia: Fortress, 1981.

Berry, Wendell. "In Distrust of Movements." *Orion* 18, no. 3 (Summer 1999) 14–18.

Boff, Leonardo. *Jesus Christ Liberator: A Critical Christology of Our Times.* Maryknoll: Orbis, 1978.

Bonhoeffer, Dietrich. *Life Together: The Classic Exploration of Faith in Community.* New York: Harper & Row, 1954.

Borat: Cultural Learnings of America for Make Benefit Glorious Nation of Kazakhstan. Directed by Larry Charles. Los Angeles: Dune Entertainment, 2006. 84 minutes.

Cavanaugh, William T. *Being Consumed: Economics and Christian Desire.* Grand Rapids: Eerdmans, 2008.

———. *Theopolitical Imagination: Discovering the Liturgy as a Political Act in an Age of Global Consumerism.* London: T. & T. Clark, 2002.

Claiborne, Shane. *The Irresistible Revolution: Living as an Ordinary Radical.* Grand Rapids: Zondervan, 2006.

———. "The Marketable Revolution." The Simple Way newsletter (March 2006). http://www.thesimpleway.org/mailings/Marchnewsletter.pdf.

Claiborne, Shane, and Chris Haw. *Jesus for President: Politics for Ordinary Radicals.* Grand Rapids: Zondervan, 2008.

Coetzee, J. M. *The Lives of Animals.* Edited and introduced by Amy Gutmann. University Center for Human Values Series. Princeton: Princeton University Press, 1999.

Colson, Charles W. "U.S. Withdrawal Morally Unacceptable Until Iraq Stable." At washingtonpost.com, January 12, 2007, On Faith. http://newsweek.washingtonpost.com/onfaith/charles_w_chuck_colson/2007/01/_there_was_a_legitimate.html.

de Gruchy, John W. *Confessions of a Christian Humanist.* Minneapolis: Fortress, 2006.

Gourevitch, Philip. *We Wish to Inform You That Tomorrow We Will Be Killed Together With Our Families.* New York: Picador, 1998.

Giddens, Anthony. *The Nation-State and Violence.* Berkeley: University of California Press, 1987.

Hall, Amy Laura. "Full House." *Christian Century* 121, no. 3 (February 10, 2004) 9–10.

———. "Unwanted Interruptions: Why Is Our Culture So Hostile to Children—Inside and Outside the Womb?" Interview by Agnieszka Tennant. *Christianity Today* 48, no. 7 (July 2004) 30–31.

Hegel, Georg Wilhelm Friedrich. *Elements of the Philosophy of Right*. Edited by Allen W. Wood. Translated by H. B. Nisbet. Cambridge Texts in the History of Political Thought. Cambridge: Cambridge University Press, 1991. Originally published as *Grundlinien der Philosophie des Rechts*, 1821.

Hinkelammert, Franz. *Cultura de la Esperanza y Sociedad sin Exclusión* (San José, Costa Rica: Departamento Ecuménico de Investigaciones, 1995.

Hirschman, Albert. *The Passions and the Interests: Political Arguments for Capitalism Before Its Triumph*. Princeton: Princeton University Press, 1981.

Hitchens, Christopher. "Kazakh Like Me." *Slate*, November 13, 2006. http://www.slate.com/id/2153578/.

Linker, Damon. *The Theocons: Secular America Under Siege*. New York: Doubleday, 2006.

Long, D. Stephen. *Divine Economy: Theology and the Market*. Radical Orthodoxy Series. New York: Routledge, 2000.

Longman, Timothy. "Christian Churches and Genocide in Rwanda." In *In God's Name: Genocide and Religion in the 20th Century*, edited by Omer Bartov and Phyllis Mack, 139–160. New York: Bergham, 2001.

MacIntyre, Alasdair C. *After Virtue: A Study in Moral Theory*. Notre Dame: University of Notre Dame Press, 1981.

———. *Marxism and Christianity*. 2nd ed. London: Duckworth, 1995.

———. *Whose Justice? Which Rationality?* Notre Dame: University of Notre Dame Press, 1987.

MacPherson, C. B. *The Political Theory of Possessive Individualism: Hobbes to Locke*. Oxford: Clarendon, 1962.

Marcuse, Herbert. *One-Dimensional Man*. Boston: Beacon, 1964.

Marsh, Charles. *Wayward Christian Soldiers: Freeing the Gospel from Political Captivity*. New York: Oxford University Press, 2007.

———. "Wayward Christian Soldiers." *The New York Times*, January 20, 2006. http://www.nytimes.com/2006/01/20/opinion/20marsh.html.

Marvin, Carolyn, and David W. Ingle. *Blood Sacrifice and the Nation: Totem Rituals and the American Flag*. Cambridge Cultural Social Studies. Cambridge: Cambridge University Press, 1999.

McCarraher, Eugene. *Christian Critics: Religion and the Impasse in Modern American Social Thought*. Ithaca, NY: Cornell University Press, 2000.

———. "Christian Intellectuals, Embedded and Otherwise." *The New Pantagruel* 1, no. 1 (Winter 2004). http://www.newpantagruel.com/issues/1.1/christian_intellectuals_embed.php.

———. "This Book is Not Good." *Commonweal*, June 15, 2007. http://www.commonwealmagazine.org/article.php3?id_article=1962.

McGarvey, Ayelish. "As God is His Witness." *The American Prospect* (October 19, 2004). http://www.prospect.org/cs/articles?articleId=8790.

McLaren, Brian. *The Church on the Other Side: Doing Ministry in the Postmodern Matrix*. Grand Rapids: Zondervan, 1998.

———. *Everything Must Change: Jesus, Global Crises, and a Revolution of Hope*. Nashville: Thomas Nelson, 2007.

———. *The Last Word and the Word After That*. San Francisco: Jossey-Bass, 2005.

———. *A New Kind of Christian: A Tale of Two Friends On A Spiritual Journey*. San Francisco: Jossey-Bass, 2001.

————. *The Secret Message of Jesus: Uncovering the Truth That Could Change Everything.* Nashville: Thomas Nelson, 2006.

Milbank, John. *Being Reconciled: Ontology and Pardon.* Radical Orthdoxy Series. New York: Routledge, 2003.

Morgan, Timothy C. "Purpose Driven in Rwanda: Rick Warren's Sweeping Plan to Defeat Poverty." *Christianity Today* 49, no. 10 (October 2005) 32–36, 90–91.

Muhamood, Mamdani. *When Victims Become Killers: Colonialism, Nativism and Genocide in Rwanda.* Princeton: Princeton University Press, 2001.

Myers, Milton L. *The Soul of Modern Economic Man: Ideas of Self Interest, Thomas Hobbes to Adam Smilty.* Chicago: University of Chicago Press, 1983.

Novak, Michael. *The Catholic Ethic and the Spirit of Capitalism.* New York: The Free Press, 1993.

————. "Changing the Paradigms: The Cultural Deficiencies of Capitalism." In *Democracy and Mediating Structures,* edited by Michael Novak, 180–200. Washington DC: American Enterprise, 1980.

————. *The Spirit of Democratic Capitalism.* New York: Touchstone, 1982.

Orzech, Charles D. "'Provoked Suicide' and the Victim's Behavior: The Case of the Vietnamese Self-Immolators." In *Curing Violence,* edited by Theophus H. Smith and Mark I. Wallace, 137–60. Forum Fascicles 3. Sonoma, CA: Polebridge, 1994.

Polkinghorne, John. *Quarks, Chaos, and Christianity.* New York: Crossroad, 2000.

Prunier, Gérard. *The Rwanda Crisis.* New York: Columbia University Press, 1995.

Rieff, Philip. *The Triumph of the Therapeutic: Uses of Faith after Freud.* New York: Harper & Row, 1966.

Sachs, Jeffrey D. *The End of Poverty: Economic Possibilities for Our Time.* New York: Penguin, 2005.

Sherman, Amy. *Preferential Option: A Christian and Neoliberal Strategy for Latin America's Poor.* Grand Rapids: Eerdmans, 1992.

Smith, Adam. *An Inquiry into the Nature and Causes of The Wealth of Nations.* Chicago: University of Chicago Press, 1976.

Sobrino, John. *Jesus the Liberator: A Historical-Theological Reading of Jesus of Nazareth.* Maryknoll: Orbis , 1993.

Volf, Miroslav. *The End of Memory: Remembering Rightly in a Violent World.* Grand Rapids: Eerdmans, 2006.

————. *Exclusion and Embrace: A Theological Exploration of Identity, Otherness, and Reconciliation.* Nashville: Abingdon, 1996.

————. *Free of Charge: Giving and Forgiving in a Culture Stripped of Grace.* Grand Rapids: Zondervan, 2006.

Volf, Miroslav, and William Katerberg. "Introduction: Reinventing Hope." In *The Future of Hope: Christian Tradition amid Modernity and Postmodernity,* edited by Miroslav Volf and William H. Katerberg, ix–xiv. Grand Rapids: Eerdmans, 2004.

Wallis, Jim. "Pro-Life Democrats?" *Sojourners* 33, no. 6 (June 2004) 5. http://www.sojo.net/index.cfm?action=magazine.article&issue=soj0406&article=040651.

Warren, Rick. *The Purpose Driven Life.* Grand Rapids: Zondervan, 2002.

Webb, Stephen H. *Good Eating: The Bible, Diet, and the Proper Love of Animals.* The Christian Practice of Everyday Life. Grand Rapids: Brazos, 2001.

————. *On God and Dogs: A Christian Theology of Compassion for Animals.* Oxford: Oxford University Press, 1998.

Wilson, John. "Be Silent—and Read My Book." *Books and Culture*, Mr. Wilson's Bookshelf, July 2, 2007. http://www.christianitytoday.com/books/features/mrwilsonsbookshelf/070702.html.

Winner, Lauren. *Real Sex: The Naked Truth About Chastity*. Grand Rapids: Brazos, 2006.

Zizioulas, John D. *Communion and Otherness: Further Studies in Personhood and the Church*. London: T. & T. Clark, 2007.